WELLBEING THROUGH U[R ... ]

# HEALT... PLACE MAKING

## FRED LONDON

RIBA Publishing

© RIBA Publishing 2020

Published by RIBA Publishing, 66 Portland Place, London, W1B 1NT

ISBN 978-1-85946-883-8

British Library Cataloguing-in-Publication Data
A catalogue record for this book is available from the British Library.

Commissioning Editor: Alexander White
Project Manager: Michèle Woodger
Production: Jane Rogers
Designed and typeset: Sara Miranda Icaza
Printed and bound by Short Run Press, Exeter
Cover: Sara Miranda Icaza

www.ribapublishing.com

FSC
www.fsc.org
MIX
Paper from
responsible sources
FSC® C014540

# ACKNOWLEDGEMENTS

Writing this book has been a very enjoyable experience, involving creative interaction with longstanding friends and colleagues, as well as with many new contacts who offered fresh information and unexpected points of view. I am extremely grateful for the time and energy that these busy people have been willing to contribute.

I am very grateful to Seppo Karppinen, director of SITO, Finland, who invited me to talk at the Annual Conference of HEPA in 2013. This inadvertently set the book in motion, via author Jonathan Tarbatt, who introduced me to RIBA commissioning editor Alex White.

Many thanks to my fellow JTP partners who have been exceptionally generous in allowing me time and space to develop my ideas, in particular Rebecca Taylor, Charles Campion and researcher Jenn Johnson, the graphics team of Adam Bowie, Joe Wood and Nat Limbrey, and Jean-Luc Jawed who designed all the diagrams.

A big thank you to Clare San Martin, Sabrina Boudalica and Joanna Allen for their clear-sighted contributions, and to Josh Cherry who helped me adapt one of his projects as a practical example. I owe the privilege of longer-term collaboration, and endless fun, to the indefatigable Debbie Radcliffe, David 'Harry-the-pencil' Harrison and the inspirational John Thompson, JTP founder chair and creator of the Academy of Urbanism (AoU).

I am most grateful for the opportunities provided by JTP's overseas collaborators, and all those contacts made during my research abroad, including: Pertti Tamminen, Kari Kankaala, Joachim Eble, Rolf Messerschmidt, Andreas von Zadow, Professor Brian Evans, Joel Mills, Jeff Tumlin, Amanda Gibbs, Joyce Drohan, Gord Price, John Stark, Charles Montgomery, Jim Diers (who introduced me to the notion of 'time banking' and 'asset-based community development'), Paddy Tillett, Al Solheim, Bill Wilson and Phil Erickson.

I derived great encouragement from contributors at the SALUS Healthy City Design International conferences, organised in 2017 and 2018 by

Marc Sansom (SALUS), jointly led by Jeremy Myerson (RCA) and the keynote of Dr Howard Frumkin (Wellcome Trust) and the presentation of Audrey de Nazelle (Imperial College London).

I am indebted to Herbert and Bettina Dreiseitl, Carl Patten, Alkis Tzavaras, Jim Diers and Kay Rood for the photographs they provided.

Returning to my editor Alex White, I am extremely thankful for his interest in the subject and belief in my ability to write about it, and for the editorial guidance of Clare Holloway and Michèle Woodger who managed the production process.

Finally, I owe a huge thank you to my dear family and friends, for their constant interest in the project and their support in helping me bring it to fruition.

# ABOUT THE AUTHOR

Fred London (MA, Dip Arch, RIBA, AoU) studied at Cambridge University Faculty of Architecture and at Harvard University Graduate School of Design, punctuated by a year of employment in Vienna. Following that, Fred joined Pollard Thomas Edwards (PTE) – where his primary focus was on social housing, later shifting his emphasis to community architecture when he joined Hunt Thompson Associates (HTA). In 1995 Fred became a founder director (now partner) of John Thompson & Partners (JTP), where he worked on numerous housing projects for developers as well as the London Wetland Centre. The scale of these projects has increased from the level of community architecture to that of community planning in the UK and Europe, as well as several international collaborations on masterplans for settlements in Russia and China. The breadth of this cross-cultural experience has contributed to a unique perspective on what makes for universally-applicable healthy placemaking.

VI

# FOREWORD
## Howard Frumkin

Once upon a time, public health and the built environment were not only contiguous territories but shared a porous border. In Britain, it was a mid-19th-century civil engineer, Joseph Bazalgette (1819-91), who gave London its sewer system, ending the city's repeated cycles of cholera, and it was an early urban epidemiologist, Edwin Chadwick (1800-90), who established the importance of housing and urban infrastructure for health. Patrick Geddes (1854-1932) – biologist, sociologist and town planner – explicitly grounded his placemaking in human needs. In the USA, Frederick Law Olmsted (1822-1903) took a break from his work designing New York's Central Park to head the US Sanitary Commission, overseeing medical care provision during the Civil War. A decade later, in 1872, the seven founders of the American Public Health Association included an architect and a housing specialist among their number.

But times have changed. Our professions have evolved and specialised. On the built environment side we have architects, city planners, landscape architects, civil engineers, transportation planners and more – graduating from distinct training programmes, earning distinct credentials, attending distinct meetings, reading different journals. On the health side we have clinical medicine and public health, each in turn divided into countless sub-fields, which function as silos. It is all too rare for a built environment professional to commune with a health professional.

However, the last two decades have seen inspiring efforts to reconnect health and the built environment. Academic research on the health implications of cities, buildings and transportation systems has blossomed. At universities there are cross-cutting courses and even degree programmes. A small but growing cadre of professionals is conversant, if not fluent, in both domains. Private firms are sensing and responding to market demand for healthy places. There are rating systems and certification schemes. Numerous articles and books have been published, aimed at both professional and general audiences. This book is a welcome addition to that corpus: RIBA and Fred London are to be commended.

As a health professional working to support this agenda, I'd offer five precepts.

First, we need to be evidence-based. The late US Senator Daniel Patrick Moynihan's famous aphorism – 'Everyone is entitled to his own opinion, but not to his own facts'– could well have been a comment on placemaking. What kinds of places are 'salutogenic' is not a matter of opinion; it is ultimately an empirical question. Health professionals and built environment professionals need to collaborate from basic research through to post-occupancy evaluations, to generate the evidence needed for valid design decision-making.

Second, never solve just one problem. Our buildings and our cities are full of unhealthy places, and we need to rectify this. But our buildings and cities are also prime culprits in the existential threat that is climate change. And our buildings and cities embody persistent, shameful, social inequities and health disparities. Healthy placemaking must also be sustainable placemaking, equitable placemaking and economical placemaking.

Third, plan ahead. Our world is changing at a velocity unprecedented in human experience. Rising temperatures, melting glaciers, disappearing species, changing weather patterns, retreating coastlines and spreading diseases are occurring not in geological time but year-on-year. With such rapid change, the past is no longer prologue to the future. That said, the general direction of travel is clear. Any building that is built, any neighbourhood that is configured, should be designed for conditions in 50 or 100 years, not for conditions that prevail today.

Fourth, define health broadly. The World Health Organization definition of health – 'a state of complete physical, mental and social well-being and not merely the absence of disease or infirmity' – is well worn but true. Yes, we need to aim for normal blood pressure, for robust lung function, for unclogged arteries. These lead to familiar mandates for the built environment, such as clean air and physical activity. But our aspirations need to be much higher. We need to avert anxiety and depression. We need to aim for life satisfaction, for happiness, for inspiration, for social connectedness, for spiritual fulfilment. Of course, healthy places cannot assure all of these outcomes. But the measure of a healthy place – indeed, the measure of a good building or a good neighbourhood or a good city – is in the end the extent to which it moves us toward these broad, aspirational outcomes.

Fifth, think of the most vulnerable. In words attributed to Mahatma Gandhi, 'the true measure of any society can be found in how it treats its most vulnerable members'. In every society, those who are poor endure some of the least healthy places: substandard housing, crumbling schools, corrosive neighbourhoods. Children need and deserve healthy places anchored in their developmental stages: clean air, protection from injury risks and toxic chemicals, ample nature contact, opportunities to play and explore. The elderly deserve much the same. People with disabilities deserve accommodations to enable them to live life to the fullest. These are all matters of simple fairness, of compassion and of collective responsibility – and are of vital interest to placemakers.

These are the perspectives of a health professional. But they are perfectly aligned with the six principles for healthy placemaking proposed in this book: urban planning, walkable communities, neighbourhood building blocks, movement networks, environmental integration and community empowerment. In fact, this alignment illustrates one of the key takeaway lessons: that a people-centred approach to the built environment, entraining the best of both health and design thinking, can work wonders for health, wellbeing and sustainability.

*Dr Howard Frumkin (MD, DrPH) is head of Our Planet Our Health at the Wellcome Trust and Professor Emeritus at the University of Washington School of Public Health. He is also former Director of the National Center for Environmental Health, US Centers for Disease Control and Prevention.*

# PREFACE

Few aspects of our lives are as precious as our health, physical and mental. Poor health can occur for a multitude of reasons but analysis shows that many risks to health are associated with the built environment. Amongst them, are concerns that public health professionals and international organisations have been working to overcome for many decades.

My own professional journey began when, free from preconceptions about where it might lead, I chose to study architecture because I enjoyed drawing and making models and wanted to learn about the subject. I studied at Cambridge from 1977-83, including a 'year out' working in Vienna, and spent the first of my diploma years on an exchange programme at the Graduate School of Design in Harvard. I then joined a practice in London that focused on mixed-use, rehab and new-build housing, primarily for public sector clients.

A trivial insight, which has nonetheless endured, occurred in 1986 when I acquired a second-hand car and used it at the weekend to go shopping in the West End. Assuming it would be easier than taking public transport or cycling, I arrived at my destination only to find myself driving away from it again. I crawled along in the traffic in search of somewhere to park, spent time procuring coins for the parking meter and walked a considerable distance back to the shop which, by then, was closing. A similar excursion a few weeks later was enough to convince me that, far from being easy, driving in central London was tiresome and frustrating.

This kind of experience got me thinking about the way we use space in cities and caused my interest in architecture to branch out towards urban planning, guided more by gut reaction than rational analysis. My fascination continued when the practice I worked for at the time – Hunt Thompson Associates – was designing new settlements and running community planning events in the UK and overseas. This gathered steam in 1995 when I became founder director (and then partner) of John Thompson & Partners, now JTP.

In the UK we facilitated public planning events working with local people, often for residential and mixed-use development projects close to where they lived. It attracted participants holding a wide variety of opinions. Some held concerns about the natural environment, some opposed new development in the belief that the addition of new homes would make the existing traffic congestion even worse and others were anxious about a lack of social infrastructure. From this came valuable insights regarding the things people find important and the many ways in which communities function.

Our collaborative masterplanning work for the mayors of cities in mainland Europe was focused on the regeneration and adaptation of whole city quarters, as opposed to the development of individual land parcels. Projects in Germany, France, Italy, Sweden, Finland and several other countries raised our awareness of broader scales of urban planning and alerted us to the differing priorities that prevailed in those places.

My thinking about what makes places healthy started to develop as a specific topic in 2001 with the EU-funded 'Ecocity' initiative, and really came to life in 2013 when I was invited to Helsinki to give a presentation at the annual conference of HEPA, a branch of the World Health Organisation. Key aims of the conference were, on the one hand, to communicate how people can lead healthier, more enjoyable lives for as long as possible, and on the other, to reduce the financial demands on overstretched health authorities caring for people suffering from lifestyle related illnesses.

HEPA stands for 'Health-Enhancing Physical Activity' and the programme of the four-day conference included numerous presentations and workshops on how to reduce obesity in children and ways in which to maintain physical activity for the elderly. Mine was one of four half-hour presentations and, after each one, the facilitators required the audience to stand up when applauding. Why? Because sitting down for too long, in this case two hours, is bad for our health. It was also noticeable how the attendees, energised in this way, were less absorbed with their smartphones, more engaged with the topics being presented and, above all, awake!

The link between HEPA's promotion of physical activity and the design of built environments is that the streets and squares that make up the public realm provide a valuable platform for daily exercise. However, exercise is just one of several aspects relevant to the healthiness of settlements. The physical dangers of traffic accidents are well known and the risks caused by poor air quality from toxic emissions are attracting increasing attention. But the built environment can also give rise to mental health issues such as loneliness and social isolation, as well as contributing to the problems caused by unhealthy diets.

With these risks and hazards recognised, the aim of healthy placemaking is to identify how best to minimise their impacts and introduce ways in which urban space can be reshaped to improve people's quality of life. This is why it is essential that designers working to make places healthier acquire a comprehensive grasp of the multifaceted concepts that need to be addressed.

Human activity taking place in built environments is bewilderingly complex and, with this in mind, I have formulated a series of interrelated but distinct principles for healthy placemaking. These reflect not only planning related matters but also the ways in which people lead their lives; how the health and wellbeing of individuals and communities can be enhanced by the choices people make, choices encouraged by carefully planned, strategic improvements to the environments in which they live.

The book is aimed not only at design professionals, but also at citizens, to arouse their interest and encourage them to contribute to the planning process.

# INTRODUCTION

## INCREASED AWARENESS

The places in which we live affect our health and wellbeing, for better or for worse. The need to rethink these environments to help us lead healthier lives began to be apparent towards the end of the 20th century, and the urgency to do so has been increasing ever since.

The many high-level, international organisations whose mission it is to combat the explosion of illnesses that result from contemporary lifestyles send out consistent messages about how we can and should lead healthier lifestyles, each one focusing on the aspects of most relevance to its specific concerns. They include the United Nations, the World Health Organisation, the National Health Service, Public Health England, Habitat, Transport for London, the Mayor's Office, The Design Council/CABE, The Royal College of Physicians, *The Lancet*, local authorities, universities, urban planners and countless other comparable organisations the world over.

A partnership of international initiatives involved with many aspects of sustainability, led by the United Nations Economic Commission for Europe and the World Health Organisation (WHO), set up the 'THE PEP'. This stands for Transport, Health, Environment Pan-European Programme, an outcome of the recognition of the massive impacts of travel on the health of our species and our planet.

The health concerns include anything from those of businesses frustrated by the loss of productivity resulting from days off work and traffic congestion, to city authorities that have woken up to the fact that the air in their streets is toxic. Coming from a different standpoint are the concerns of the UK's admirable but overstretched National Health Service (NHS) which could function much more effectively and economically if relieved of the burden of treating sicknesses and deaths caused by lifestyle-generated illnesses.

We need to find ways to overcome the complex train of societal developments that have led to these problems. The encouraging news is that widespread research and analysis are raising our understanding, and the media is communicating what needs to be done. At grassroots level the responses to the proposed solutions vary across a broad spectrum from acceptance to denial, perhaps because there are so many issues to take on board and none of them offer quick results.

However, healthy placemaking – rather than being a question of 'silver bullet' remedies that reliably deliver benefits – lies instead in a series of six interrelated principles set out in the central chapters of this book. Individually, none of these principles will give rise to major improvements, but their combined effect contributes to environments that create the conditions for people to lead healthier lives.

This approach is important in three ways:

1. It recognises that many environments in which we live are not healthy places, and therefore interventions to improve them are not merely desirable, but essential; a message that is endorsed and communicated by governments, health authorities and pressure groups around the world.

2. Places created following the principles outlined in this book cannot in themselves cause those who live, work, learn and play in them to become healthier, but can create the conditions in which barriers to positive health outcomes are minimised, and opportunities to lead healthier lives are created.

   To some degree it depends on whether individuals are inclined to take these opportunities. For those motivated or able to take them the choices are available – meanwhile those less motivated can be encouraged to try them out. But the central plank of the healthy placemaking strategy is to assume that not enough of us will follow the guidance on offer, so the emphasis needs to be on introducing measures that will help us to lead healthier lives without necessarily having made a conscious effort to do so, or even being aware that we have succeeded.

3. There are huge health inequalities in urgent need of rebalancing, from country to country and within every country too, but the focus of healthy placemaking is on the reduction of poor health caused directly

or indirectly, and knowingly or unknowingly, by our chosen lifestyles. 'Avoidable illnesses' is the term frequently used by the health services that treat them, and those who suffer from these afflictions may come from a wide variety of backgrounds, crossing boundaries of wealth, class and education.

There are many causes of avoidable illnesses that cannot be influenced directly by urban planning strategies, such as substance abuse, smoking and unhealthy diets. But in encouraging healthy lifestyles for everyone through carefully curated environments, healthy placemaking will also reach people who struggle with these damaging habits.

## HIGHER ASPIRATIONS

In its 1948 constitution, the WHO defined health in its broader sense as 'a state of complete physical, mental, and social wellbeing and not merely the absence of disease or infirmity'.[1]

The WHO's distinction between being genuinely healthy, as opposed to not being ill, provides an ideal starting point for this book, in reminding us that the experience of true quality of life requires us to aim higher than just getting by.

Many illnesses can be cured but preventing them is better. In WHO terms, the aim of health is for it to last throughout our lives at as high a level as possible. This is all the more relevant as modern medicine has increased longevity worldwide, with global average life expectancy having increased by 5.5 years between 2000 and 2016.[2] This is only genuinely good news if we enjoy a good quality of life in those additional years, without imposing undue and unaffordable burdens on our families, friends and health services.

The onset of deteriorating health with age, that affects everyone, can be delayed by lifestyle choices that extend healthy longevity. But perhaps people take it for granted that the medical profession – with its incredibly high standards of care and cure – will be there to pick up the pieces if they overstep the mark?

The most immediate priority for health professionals is to identify and treat the diseases from which we suffer; the primary focus of their essential work remains within the realm of illness. However, this can be complemented by an approach that focuses instead on creating conditions that enable us to enjoy a wider sense of wellbeing and an enhanced quality of life. This is a form of preventative medicine that has nothing to do with medical intervention but can still support good practice. Its emphasis is on areas not immediately regarded as issues of public health but are nonetheless of immense value in avoiding illness by enhancing wellbeing.

Things we experience and respond to in our environments can improve our health by inducing feelings of happiness: when we find things beautiful, surprising, interesting, stimulating, comforting, new, amusing or downright funny, it raises our spirits. There are many organisations that report on the benefits of happiness, including the Harvard School of Public Health, Healthline and the USA's National Academy of Sciences. *The Greater Good; the Science of a Meaningful Life* sets out its 'Six Ways Happiness Is Good for Your Health',[3] reporting that happiness protects your heart, strengthens your immune system, minimises stress, reduces aches and pains, combats disease and disability and lengthens our lives.

This book aims to set out how the environments in which we live have influenced our health and wellbeing and the ways we can adapt these environments to offer us healthier lifestyles that can improve our individual and collective quality of life.

## CONNECTED STRATEGIES

Prioritising the long-term health of people of all ages and from all walks of life is essential, and all the more urgent as populations continue to live longer. When trying to implement strategies to adapt our environment for better health, some aspects can be 'easy wins' whilst others are harder to introduce. This is particularly true in the face of resistance from individuals and organisations intent on continuing with their business models despite the damage they are known to cause to human health, and that of the environment. A typical scenario is when a specific problem is resolved by adjustments, followed by a quick return to 'business as usual'.

For example, the direct connection between the widespread use of motor vehicles in our busy cities and the poor air quality experienced by all of us who spend time in them is becoming an increasing concern. An example of a response to this is the Mayor of London's introduction of the Ultra-Low Emission Zone (ULEZ), a decision which met with backlash from businesses who experienced immediate inconveniences, but was considered hugely valuable for the long-term health benefits. A publication by the Royal College of Physicians (RCP), 'Every breath we take: the lifelong impact of air pollution', explores the effects on different generations: 'As children, today's grandparents were exposed to soot and sulphur dioxide from coal burning. Those now in middle age breathed in emissions from leaded petrol. Today's children walk and cycle much less, and they inhale nitrogen dioxide and the tiny particulates from diesel-fuelled vehicles.'[4] The RCP's point is expanded upon with the warning that 'Around the world, there are many examples where reducing air pollution has improved public health. It now seems likely that childhood exposure to air pollution has a lasting influence on health, so the gains from tackling air pollution today will be felt throughout the decades to come.'[5]

To say that air quality problems caused by fossil fuel vehicle emissions in cities can be overcome by replacing them with electric cars may seem positive but it is far from being a complete solution, as we would still inhale the dangerous dust particles given off by the brakes and tyres of electric vehicles. This is why we need to take a higher-level stance to deliver connected strategies as opposed to one-off solutions to individual problems. The complexity of our lives and the number of 'scares' reported in the news every day mean that it would be easier for us to take them on board if we understood that so many of the issues are interrelated and fall under the single umbrella of healthy placemaking.

We must comprehend that adjustments to the urban structure to make it friendlier for pedestrians would address several health issues at one stroke; improving air-quality, making the public realm safer and more attractive, and increasing the numbers of us getting more exercise in daily life. It would generate an increase in the social interaction that helps to unite communities, enhance our sense of wellbeing and would have a good chance of boosting local economies.

If we as individuals and as part of a global society had already explored every option to remedy the problems we face, we would be in a much worse predicament. But countless stones remain unturned and only a fraction of them will need to be explored, understood and acted upon to effect sweeping improvements.

We must sustain this approach by our will and determination to take it as a matter of the utmost importance; from the grassroots to the highest levels of government.

## CHAPTER 1

# HUMAN NATURE AND HEALTH

*'Tackling pollution and promoting active travel through compact cities also creates the right environment for physical activity. In our sedentary societies, increased levels of physical activity have proven health benefits for adults and children, reducing a number of chronic and cardiovascular diseases.'*[1]

**LAURENCE CARMICHAEL**

This chapter describes how the combination of societal progress and medical expertise has given rise to new health challenges that result from the 21st-century lifestyles to which we have become accustomed and take for granted. It points to the inconsistency of our behaviour in terms of how we deal with health issues in our daily lives and the relationship between human health and the health of the planet.

# WE HAVE COME A LONG WAY

As we enter a food store, full of extraordinary produce from all over the world that we can take home in our cars, do we give a thought as to how much more difficult that process was only a few generations back?

Life for *Homo sapiens* has undergone fundamental transformations, from hunting and gathering subsistence to today's hi-tech lifestyles. Developments include the establishment of agriculture, the growth of large settlements and the expansion of trade over ever-increasing distances – typically accompanied by exploitation, conflict and war.

Many jobs were extremely dangerous in bygone eras, when neither health and safety nor reasonable working hours were considered relevant and, as a result, life expectancies were correspondingly shorter. What doctors could do to cure the sick and wounded in the past was limited compared to the extraordinary medical knowledge of today.

In 1800s Great Britain, increasingly sophisticated agrarian economies paved the way for the Industrial Revolution. Rapid migration from rural to urban environments ensued, giving rise to unprecedented challenges, such as overcrowded housing, slums and poor sanitation in towns and cities.

The scourge of cholera was one of the biggest health problems in London until its source was identified and analysed by physician John Snow in 1854; this led to the installation of clean water systems across the developed world.

The direction of urban planning was transformed by pioneering work in the 19th and 20th centuries that produced new systems and choices for mobility. Philanthropic movements recognised the extreme social problems resulting from exploitative labour practices, and the poor health suffered by those living in woefully unhygienic conditions. One response was to fund the provision of (generally) well-built urban housing. Another was to propose new kinds of settlement where people could live and work in greener, healthier environments.

In the early phases of such initiatives, these settlements were intended to be accessed by public transport, primarily trains and underground railways. In 1898, Ebenezer Howard established the Garden City Movement, which offered oppressed employees and their families a better chance in life. This, and the rise of suburbia, was made possible by growing rail transport networks. Almost a century later, in the 1970s, this concept still played a large part in the marketing of London's Tube system, which invited residents to 'Come to Ruislip, where the air is fine, it's only half-an-hour on the Piccadilly Line'.[2]

As settlements grew, transport became of increasing importance – the rail network being only one development of many. In 1890s London and New York the authorities were also struggling to dispose of vast quantities of manure left by tens of thousands of carriage horses. One remedy was the 'horseless carriage' – the early automobile. This would become the dominant force in 20th-century urban planning.

In terms of medical advancement, by the mid-20th century the UK started to benefit from spectacular improvements in medicine, whereby many previously fatal conditions became curable, and healthcare became widely accessible thanks to the establishment of the NHS in 1948. Progress was also made with better housing conditions, availability of healthier food and a raft of social reforms, including health and safety at work, that improved people's quality of life.

But since the latter part of the 20th century, along with a well-deserved sense of achievement for these magnificent medical advances, there is also growing awareness that the amount we consume, and the ease of the lives we lead, create health problems of a different complexion. Many of these are attributable to lifestyles that have arisen as a consequence of the way our cities are planned.

## SOME PROBLEMS ARE NOT NEW

The introductory pages of the 1945 *County of London Plan*, under the heading 'What is Wrong' (written as a statement rather than as a question), announces in emotive terms: 'The [London Plan] Report lists four defects: Traffic congestion, depressed housing, inadequacy and maldistribution of open spaces and, finally, the jumble of houses and industry. An additional fifth defect is the continued sprawl of London ribboning along the roads, straggling over the Home Counties and suburbanising the whole of the surrounding country towns.'[3] The case is reinforced by the caption of an aerial view of a mixed-use neighbourhood describing it as the 'muddled use of land'.

Prepared whilst WW2 was coming to an end, this fascinating document reflects Modernism's hallmark optimism for a rational, scientific future. In that climate it is unsurprising that 'the jumble of houses and industry' and 'muddled use of land' would be regarded as one of the many 'defects' in need of rationalisation.

Subsequent experience has given us a more nuanced understanding of industry, separating out the uses that can be hazardous whilst allowing the integration of 'people-friendly' forms of employment whose proximity to residential areas contributes to what we would now regard as an entirely positive 'jumble' of uses.

This *County of London Plan*, that inspired mid 20th-century Modernism in architecture and urban planning in the UK, treated the car as an icon for the Machine Age. Speed was the attraction, and creating the conditions for the car to be used at speed was what preoccupied the planners. Anything that might get in the way of the speeding car was to be banished from the road: 'Fast cars must be able to move fast and be segregated from lorries and buses… However perfect the roads themselves may be, if they are interrupted by crossings – or crossroads – they will not be able to *fulfil their function.*'[4]

This is a prescient description of what we have long-since called a motorway. Next to the heading: 'The Problem of Speed is relatively new to the town planner; it dates from the advent of the motor car' is a charming diagram showing that pedestrians move at 3 mph, horse-drawn carriages at 5 mph, bicycles at 8 mph and cars at 60 mph.[5] The 60 mph remains accurate enough in terms of motorway driving but traffic in cities has always averaged circa 10 mph which reinforces the idea that cities may not be the ideal places for cars 'to fulfil their function'.

To repeat the statement 'What is Wrong', three quarters of a century later, the most obvious 'defect' is that the innumerable benefits offered by the private car have become so ingrained in our habits and consciousness that it is hard to distinguish the circumstances under which they cease to be an asset and start to be a liability. The extracts quoted above show that certain problems were already a major cause for concern in the 1940s; a salutary reminder of how long society has been grappling, unsuccessfully, with this challenge.

In the same way that the 1940s catered to the icon of the automobile, it is of the utmost importance that planners and designers now work towards adapting existing places and creating new ones that allow people the best opportunity to 'fulfil their function' – of leading their lives in environments planned to maximise health and wellbeing.

## ATTITUDES TO HEALTH

### WHAT ARE AVOIDABLE ILLNESSES?

The experience of wellbeing, of feeling healthy, of enjoying good health, is of immense value – but is something too often regarded as normal, taken for granted until people feel unwell. Many illnesses and injuries, both minor and serious, arise from circumstances that could not have been prevented. But the ailments variously referred to by health professionals as 'avoidable' or 'preventable illnesses' or 'noncommunicable diseases' (NCDs) are those that often result from choices that people have made, or that the circumstances of their lives have dictated to them. Lifestyle choices on a personal level often lead to the illnesses that damage health, but there is a broader responsibility for planners and designers to shoulder some of this responsibility by making healthy alternatives available, and encouraging their use.

The most prevalent illnesses are cardiovascular diseases, type 2 diabetes, many cancers, respiratory illnesses and mental health problems. Research indicates that aspects of urban life can be a contributory factor to all of these illnesses. Added to this list are transport related accidents, for which being 'avoidable' has different connotations.

Many avoidable illnesses are associated with long-term sedentary lifestyles, so overcoming the ingrained habits that caused them can be a long-term undertaking, requiring determination and persistence.

Table 1.1 sets out the main health problems that people suffer from, their causes and how to address them, followed by explanations and supporting evidence to substantiate the claims:

| MAIN HEALTH PROBLEMS | Cardiovascular disease, type 2 diabetes, and obesity; several forms of cancer (referred to as 'avoidable illnesses') | | Respiratory diseases, including asthma | Mental illnesses | Transport related accidents |
|---|---|---|---|---|---|
| CAUSES | Sedentary lifestyles and lack of exercise | Poor diet and food poverty | Poor air quality | Loneliness, isolation, limited social interaction and fear of crime | Interaction of vehicles with cyclists and pedestrians |
| ADDRESSING THE CAUSES | Enable exercise in daily life | Provide education, accessible facilities and available green spaces | Limit the causes and effects of vehicular emissions | Community facilities and safe, sociable, productive environments | Good urban and transport design |

**TABLE 1.1**
Main lifestyle related health problems, their causes and how to address them

## 1. ENABLE EXERCISE IN DAILY LIFE

Defining the situation in uncompromising terms, *The Lancet's* September 2016 report 'City Planning and population health: a global challenge' states that: 'In high-income countries, time in cars, television viewing, and other screen use account for up to 85% of adults' non-occupational sitting time. Worldwide, sedentary behaviours are rapidly rising as LMIC [Low and Middle-income Countries] shift from agricultural to manufacturing and service economies with increased use of labour-saving devices and more motorised forms of transport.'[6] This behavioural change could indicate a rapid increase in cases of the avoidable illnesses listed above, and put further pressure on already stretched health services.

The WHO's 'Global action plan on physical activity 2018–2030' responds to the situation, stating that 'Regular physical activity is proven to help prevent and treat noncommunicable diseases (NCDs) such as heart disease, stroke, diabetes and breast and colon cancer. It also helps to prevent hypertension, overweight and obesity and can improve mental health, quality of life and wellbeing.'[7] This is a recurring theme that is well known to a significant percentage of the population but for whom taking concerted action to overcome it is nonetheless lacking.

## 2. PROVIDE EDUCATION, ACCESSIBLE FACILITIES AND AVAILABLE GREEN SPACES

The Food Foundation is an independent think-tank that tackles the growing challenges facing the UK's food system in the interests of the UK public. Its recent analysis shows that the food environment makes it too difficult for typical British families to choose a healthy diet.

Healthy foods can be up to three times more expensive than unhealthy foods. Families spend nearly a fifth (18%) of their budget on food but throw away the equivalent of six meals per week. Highly processed foods which can be damaging to health make up over half the diet of typical families. Almost all of a child's daily sugar allowance is contained in one UK leading-brand yoghurt, yet is cheaper than a plain natural yoghurt. Advertising of foods high in fat, sugar and salt is unregulated and widespread during family TV viewing times, as well as throughout the internet. The number of places to eat out has grown by more than 50% over the last ten years but many serve unhealthy meals.

Over half of adults are overweight and obese, 5% have diabetes and one third of five year olds have tooth decay. The UK has the third highest rates of obesity in the EU and rates are still increasing. Our diets are too high in saturated fat and sugar and too low in fibre, notably fruit and vegetables. There is a very significant wealth gradient in consumption of fruit and vegetables – the poorest 10% of households only purchase 3.2 portions of fruit and vegetables per day.[8]

In January 2019, the Environmental Audit Committee published its latest report on the *Sustainable Development Goals in the UK* follow-up: 'Hunger, malnutrition and food insecurity in the UK'.[9] The major findings were that food insecurity is significant and growing in the UK, with levels among the worst in Europe, especially for children. It reports that the government has failed to recognise and respond domestically and has allowed these issues to 'fall between the cracks'. The government's obesity strategy is silent on food insecurity and the report highlights the need to ensure government cross-departmental understanding and action on hunger, to implement strategies for improvement and to monitor progress.

Food poverty relates to the unaffordable cost of food that is available and also the lack of accessibility of food that is healthy, as retailers may not wish to open outlets in poorer neighbourhoods. Urban planning can play a role, with the help of local authorities, in providing facilities where citizens can learn about the importance of healthy diets and potentially have access to gardens, green spaces or allotments where they can grow their own food.

Access to good quality green space is beneficial in guarding against cardiovascular disease and type 2 diabetes and several forms of cancer. This is due to the benefits of exercise outdoors in clean air and the enjoyment of contact with nature and social interaction.

### 3. LIMIT THE CAUSES AND EFFECTS OF VEHICULAR EMISSIONS

In recent decades, media coverage of the lamentable state of the air quality in many of our towns and cities has led to a sharp rise in public awareness. The RCP reports that 'Each year in the UK, around 40,000 deaths are attributable to exposure to outdoor air pollution'.[10]

A significant proportion of the toxins discharged in urban streets are from motor vehicles emitting poisonous fumes right next to people on pavements, and this impacts everyone spending time outdoors in the public realm. It is essentially 'unavoidable' for local residents, pedestrians, cyclists and drivers who breathe it. The only sense in which it can be regarded as 'avoidable' is that it may not have been necessary or desirable for those vehicles to have been driven into busy urban spaces in the first place. Those experiencing the highest levels of unhealthy air are not the pedestrians and cyclists but the drivers themselves, in the enclosed space of their vehicles: 'Pollutant levels are often higher inside because cars take in emissions from surrounding vehicles and recirculate them.'[11]

The High Court recently granted a new inquest into the death of a nine-year-old schoolgirl who died in 2013 of an asthma attack thought to be linked to illegal levels of air pollution near her south London home, 25 m from the South Circular road in Lewisham.

According to the report in the Guardian, nearly 40 million people in the UK live in areas with illegal levels of air pollution, and judges have repeatedly condemned the government for failing to tackle levels of nitrogen dioxide from diesel vehicles.[12] Air pollution has been measured at illegal levels in 37 out of 43 zones across the country.

### 4. COMMUNITY FACILITIES AND SAFE, SOCIABLE, PRODUCTIVE ENVIRONMENTS

The social value of communities is well understood. In Frome, Somerset, Helen Kingston, an innovative GP, has taken this to a new level by instituting the 'Compassionate Frome Project', aimed at 'building a more compassionate community', based on 'knowing what is available in the community and filling in the gaps'.[13]

Kingston's 2016 report, along with the Guardian article of 2018,[14] describes the many aspects that were brought together to make Compassionate Frome possible. Urban planning can support such initiatives indirectly by highlighting the need for local authorities to fund facilities for social care and community engagement.

### 5. GOOD URBAN AND TRANSPORT DESIGN

The minimisation of transport related accidents depends on the way road networks are laid out and managed. The many users of the public realm compete for space and the larger and more powerful vehicles present greater risks to the more vulnerable ones. Key issues are for speeds to be not only limited but also observed, as accidents involving vehicles travelling at 20 mph or slower are significantly less likely to end in fatalities.

This list of avoidable illnesses and the measures that aim to address them are summarised here and will be explained further in the chapters to come. They will set designers the challenge to create environments that make it easier for people to do what will be good for their short-term and long-term health. Adopting this approach will be beneficial to everyone, all of the time, regardless of how healthy or unhealthy they may be.

## NATURAL ATTRACTIONS OF THE 'EASY LIFE'

Faced with emergencies or acute medical conditions people act immediately to avert personal and/or collective disaster. But, absorbed in the here and now, they may postpone or ignore action that would benefit their health in the long term. For many, thinking about how their current lifestyles could have negative effects in the future is not a priority.

It can be hard to resist tasty but unhealthy food and drink, or getting into the car to travel even short distances. But both of these choices can lead to a downward spiral whereby an unbalanced diet and a lack of regular exercise means people can find it tiring to walk for more than a short distance. Having reached this stage, it is hard for them to imagine that exercise, rather than being an activity engaged in by masochists, can be a natural and pleasurable experience they may not even notice they are doing.

The 'London Travel Demand Survey' statistics reporting that '3.6 million car journeys are made by Londoners every day (2 million of those are under 2 km)' may reflect how many of us shy away from walking distances that may take only 15–20 minutes on foot or 5–8 minutes by bicycle.[15]

Figure 1.1 is a simple way to illustrate how people may react to the situations that characterise their daily lives. These may be to do with what they eat and drink, how they spend free time, the ways they get about – for work, family matters or shopping – and their attitude to getting the recommended levels of daily exercise. According to the NHS, people should have at least 150 minutes of moderate exercise a week, as well as strength-building exercise on two or more days.[16]

The diagram proposes four outcomes that arise when the activities that people like or dislike doing are combined with those that are good or bad for their health. For example, people's lives can be easier if they like taking exercise or, if they do not enjoy it, they may choose to do it anyway because they understand the long-term benefits. To neglect daily exercise due to finding it disagreeable is a choice that may be regretted sooner or later. Being forced to work beyond what is healthy, perhaps through working in a polluted environment or subjected to an excess of physical labour, denotes unfairness.

That final category of 'no choice' may mean that those affected by an unfair scenario require support from external sources. For the other three, each person will strike a balance regarding the importance of maintaining their health whilst accommodating the numerous choices they make in daily life that influence their overall sense of wellbeing in the shorter and longer term.

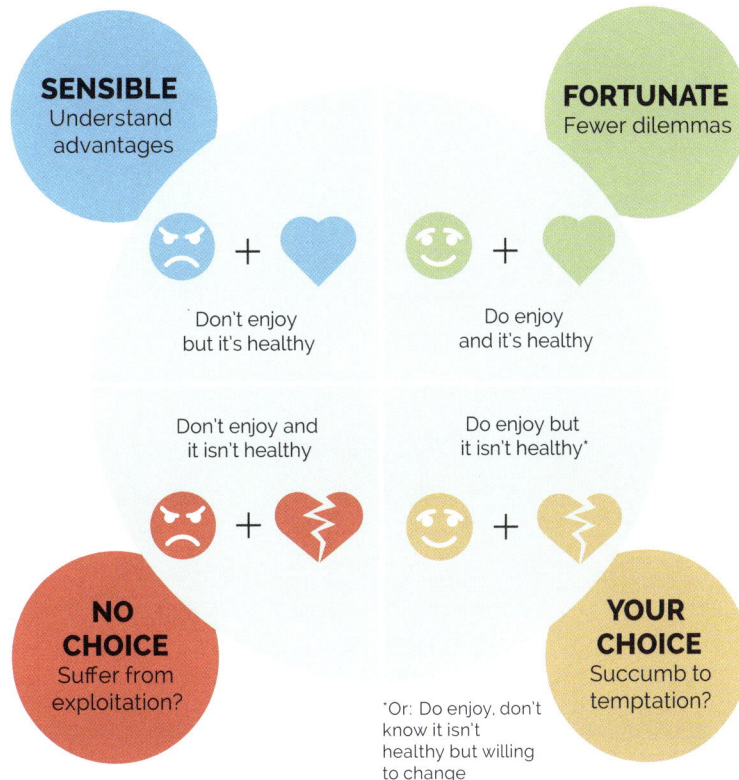

**SENSIBLE**
Understand advantages

Don't enjoy but it's healthy

**FORTUNATE**
Fewer dilemmas

Do enjoy and it's healthy

Don't enjoy and it isn't healthy

Do enjoy but it isn't healthy*

**NO CHOICE**
Suffer from exploitation?

**YOUR CHOICE**
Succumb to temptation?

*Or: Do enjoy, don't know it isn't healthy but willing to change

**FIGURE 1.1**
Life's choices

## OUR CHANGING LIFESTYLES

Finding ways to get about was an integral part of our lives even before we evolved into *Homo sapiens*. Anthropologists have shown that the edge we had in hunting down live prey was a combination of intelligence, cooperation and endurance running. The success of our early primate ancestors resulted from the sweat they were able to discharge due to their lack of fur. This enabled them to wear down faster-running animals whose dense fur caused them to collapse from heat exhaustion.[17]

The human inventiveness that gave rise to growing crops and rearing animals was, as a lifestyle, less energetic than hunter-gathering and was a primary influence on the development of communal settlements and the specialisation of skills. The result was that long-distance running ceased to be a necessity but, although we still possess the genes that endow us with these qualities, contemporary lifestyles mean that we rarely need to use them, or have to make a special effort to do so.

The disadvantage of having too little exercise is encapsulated in the saying 'use it or lose it', which refers to the need for people to keep their physiognomies active to avoid them wasting away. The fact that so many do not 'use it' enough leads to poor physical health; hence the widespread concern amongst health professionals, local authorities and governments.

Physical activities and challenges play an important part in keeping our minds and bodies functioning properly; 'It can reduce your risk of major illnesses, such as heart disease, stroke, type 2 diabetes and cancer by up to 50% and lower your risk of early death by up to 30%.'[18]

Resistance to performing an activity which may seem like unnecessary exertion is natural, so one of the best ways for people to get the exercise needed for long-term health is for it to be integral to their daily lives, and the design of settlements can encourage this.

The good news is that the 'use it or lose it' principle no longer depends on our running long distances, as it is surprising how little is actually needed to make a difference. Walking is enough, because, provided it is on a regular basis, even relatively low-intensity use of our limbs accustoms our bodies to the exercise we need and exertion soon ceases to feel unwelcome or to be avoided.

The simple and fundamentally human activity of walking, which is part of our genetic make-up, turns out to be a force to be reckoned with. In terms of transport it is known as 'active travel' because, quite simply, it requires exertion. Cycling and the use of scooters of course also qualify as active travel, as do any journeys by bus, tram, train, taxi or car club vehicle, as we have to walk to make use of them. Designers must work to encourage active travel in their plans to counter the problem of car dependency, which is a leading contributor to many 'avoidable' illnesses. In many areas, car dependency is inevitable because the design of the town allows for no alternative activity. Brent Toderian points out that 'car dependency is a leading contributor to the epidemic of preventable diseases that are linked to how we design our cities. We have created obesogenic environments that are literally killing us... We've designed daily, ordinary activity out of our lives. The costs and consequences aren't just to us as individuals, they're to all of us as taxpayers.'[19]

Standing is another active choice that should not be underestimated. 'HEPA', an acronym that stands for 'Health Enhancing Physical Activity', was set up in 2004 as a branch of the WHO. It has been responding to inconvenient truths about health by finding ways to encourage physical activity across the generations. During part of its annual conference in 2013, the HEPA facilitator requested the audience to stand up when applauding each speaker. The knowledgeable attendees were well aware of the health benefits these simple actions would offer them, not only as part of their long-term health strategy but also in keeping them awake and engaged for the duration of the presentations.

Parents often choose to protect young children by taking them to primary school by car, particularly when it is raining. But this may not be serving the interests of the short- or long-term health of their charges as it not only deprives the youngsters of daily exercise that would help to guard them from gaining too much weight but also delivers them to what is often a hectic drop-off area where they are surrounded by exhaust fumes. This is highlighted by the RCP, pointing out that 'Infants are relatively immobile and dependent on their parents to protect them or move them from sources of pollution, yet their main mode of outdoor transport seems designed to put them at precisely the level of motor vehicle exhaust emissions.'[20]

**FIGURE 1.2**
At the HEPA conference in 2013, delegates were asked to stand up to improve their health

By contrast, clad in wet-weather gear and walking along a footpath far enough away from a busy road for the air to be fairly clean, the children can learn the route and how to cross roads and are likely to enjoy experiencing the elements and splashing in puddles.

The good news is that many local authorities across the UK are banning drop-off and pick-up by car at primary school gates. The charity 'Living Streets' has introduced the 'Park and Stride' strategy whereby the last 10 minutes of the children's journey to school is on foot, either by the car being parked some distance away or by getting out of the bus or tram one or two stops early. As Kathryn Shaw, from Living Streets, pointed out: 'When parents drive up to the school gates, it's not just their children they're dropping off for the day. The toxic fumes from the cars stay too. A lot of parents don't want to drive all the way but feel there is no other option.'[21]

School drop-off areas take up significant amounts of space that is used for perhaps half an hour twice a day and not at all at weekends or during school holidays. Now that this is being understood there is scope for the space to be used in many other ways.

The 'Walking Bus' is another approach that offers valuable health benefits to youngsters, explained in more detail in Chapter 3.5, *Environmental Integration*.

## HEALTHY PLANET

In his keynote speech 'Our Planet, our Health, our Cities' at the SALUS Healthy City Design conference in October 2018, Dr Howard Frumkin's fundamental message was that 'Humans can't be healthy on a planet that isn't healthy'.[22]

With the focus on the creation of environments that will be beneficial to human health there can be a blind spot regarding the health of the planet as a whole, as if the two realms are distinct from one another. It must, however, be self-evident that for living organisms to be healthy, including humans, it is essential for there to be a healthy natural environment of air, water and soil that is clean and can support the ecological biodiversity that maintains the health of the planet.

Humankind's rapid consumption of natural resources causes pollution that harms delicate global ecosystems. We have already established that air pollution is toxic to our bodies, but it is also a significant cause of climate change, putting food, air and water supplies at risk and threatening our health and wellbeing. If we do not take action against it now, the effects both on our health and that of the environment will continue to worsen.

This is emphasised in the RCP's report 'Every breath we take' which states that 'Many of the pollutants that cause this environmental damage are the same ones that are toxic to our bodies. These health problems will get worse if we continue on our current course'.[23] Despite decades of awareness about the unsustainable, destructive action that the human race has been inflicting on irreplaceable resources, environmental calamity is staring us in the face. The natural resources are infinitely precious in themselves, and the future of *Homo sapiens* depends on them. But the barely-checked expansionism, acquisitiveness and environmental destruction resulting from the wasteful consumption of ever-increasing populations of humans show that short-termism still holds sway.

The exponential rise of $CO_2$ emissions in the last few decades is at the heart of the problems as the design of our cities has led to the global use of fossil fuel vehicles. *The Lancet* explores this issue, stating 'The transport sector indirectly affects health through climate change pathways by accounting for 25% of global carbon dioxide emissions; 75% of which arise from road transport.'[24]

Whilst the worst damage to date is limited to extremely unfortunate areas around the globe, fear for the future is a massive concern, now referred to as 'eco-anxiety', especially as the prognoses of climate change continue to worsen. In the Stern Review of 2006 on 'The Economics of Climate Change', economist Nicholas Stern stated that the impacts of climate change on the global economy would be extremely serious, but he qualified this comment saying: 'This is a major challenge, but sustained long-term action can achieve it at costs that are low in comparison to the risks of inaction.'[25]

Such action as has been taken in the intervening years has been far below what was recommended and required. Yet ten years after Stern's review, the RCP still has a positive outlook and suggests that with immediate action we still have the chance to save our own health and the future of our planet.[26]

## CHAPTER 2

# HEALTH
## AT THE HEART OF
# PLANNING

*'These conversations are linked into a sort of unified theory of urbanism: simple things like multimodal design for walking, biking, and transit; mixed land use; and designing and building great places. Those ideas resonate with most people, and most politicians. There's just a lot of momentum built into the status quo.'*[1]

**BRENT TODERIAN**

# INTRODUCTION

This chapter sets out the ways in which urban planning can address the health issues faced in current society and how planners and designers can create environments that will help to prevent avoidable illnesses at an early stage. Progress is being made in many areas, but not enough people have the confidence to make decisions to safeguard their long-term health. So, designers need to develop an understanding of how to create the spatial conditions that facilitate healthy choices by setting out the underlying principles that inform the key issues.

Whereas Chapter 1 set out the health challenges of addressing avoidable illnesses, Chapter 2 looks at health from a different perspective. It considers the same challenges but explores them in terms of seven separate but interconnected 'health targets' that can enable people's lives to be led healthily. It then continues with the advantages of healthy procurement processes for design projects and the benefits of participatory planning as a desirable methodology for creating places healthily, for which the community's involvement is a key factor in the way they were conceived and designed.

# ECOCITY

A useful starting point is 'Ecocity', an initiative documented by an international team between 2002 and 2005 and sponsored by the EU, with a brief to produce best-practice principles and preliminary designs for urban planning projects in seven European cities, as far apart as Barcelona in Spain to Tampere in Finland. The process involved workshops in the cities of the participating countries with the focus on sustainable masterplanning. One of the end results is illustrated in Figure 2.1, a seminal Venn diagram consisting of four overlapping principles of Ecocity planning:

- urban structure
- energy and material flows
- transport
- socio-economic issues.

**URBAN STRUCTURE**

Minimise Greenfield consumption

**TRANSPORT**

Minimise primary energy consumption

Minimise transport demand

Minimise primary material and energy consumption

Satisfy basic needs

Minimise impairment of environment and human health

Maximise mental wellbeing and community feeling

Realise structures for human care

Create a framework for good governance

**ENERGY AND MATERIAL FLOWS**

Maximise awareness to sustainable development

Realise a diversified, crisis-resistant, local innovative economy

Minimise total costs

**CONTEXT**

Maximise respect natural + anthropogenic context

Interaction with regional + municipal material flows

**SOCIO-ECONOMIC ISSUES**

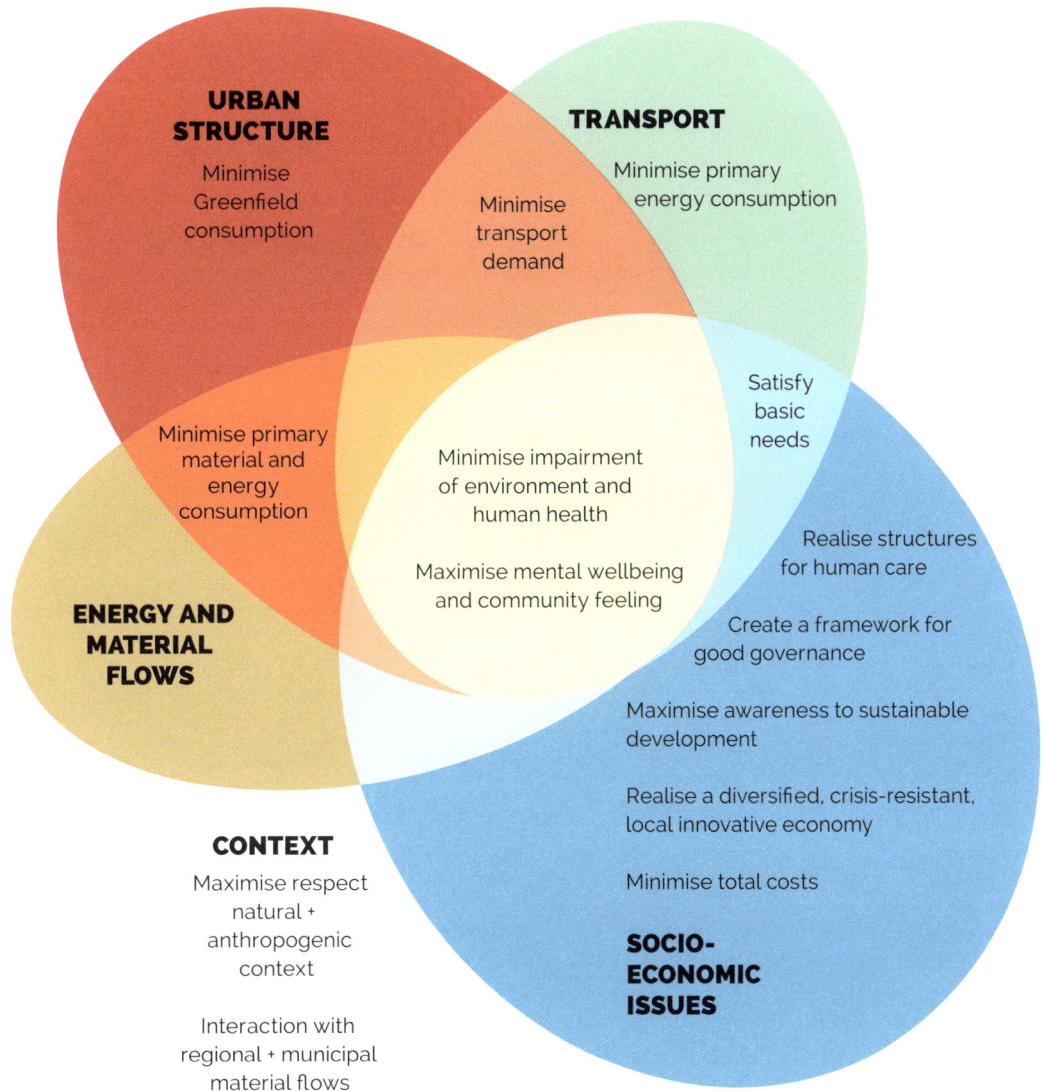

**FIGURE 2.1** Ecocity diagram

Of particular relevance are two statements in the central field where all four elements overlap and whose sole content refers to aspects of health:

- minimise impairment of environment and human health; and
- maximise mental wellbeing and community feeling.

Most similar documents that deal with these topics refer to public health as an objective alongside others. So, the selection of environment, physical and mental health and community to occupy the place where the four functional elements intersect has the effect of elevating health and wellbeing to the highest status and prioritising them as the most important goals for human life.

The Ecocity approach would require adjustments to ways of life to which people would need to become accustomed. To some, the idea of prioritising health may be seen as a threat to other aspects of life but, over time, progress is being made and key issues are becoming better understood, so it makes sense both to introduce and disseminate these concepts amongst built-environment professionals and to the wider public. One of the biggest obstacles is the understandable fear that the changes being suggested will lower the quality of our lives, whereas the fact is that the entire focus of those changes, and of this book, is to raise it.

## CITIES GROWING HEALTHILY

Towns and cities are founded and grow for many reasons. Whilst the health of their citizens may have been a key consideration at the time of their foundation, the degree to which that objective was maintained will have undergone change due to countless societal and technological developments as places have been adapted over the centuries. Overall, the process can be seen as one of continual, positive innovation, but some of the systems introduced have turned out to be detrimental to public health.

As mentioned in Chapter 1, the expertise of the medical profession has been on a gradual learning curve whose trajectory has been rising ever faster in conquering the causes of sickness and mortality. This process of research and analysis has revealed that many of the areas where public health has shortcomings are associated with the way settlements have been planned.

This in turn has highlighted the fact that new habits have been assimilated resulting from urban planning decisions designed to serve us, which in themselves may be seen as enhancements to our quality of life, but are giving rise to unintended consequences that are damaging to our health.

The growing awareness, as in Figure 2.1, that the health of individuals, families, communities and nations should be treated as a top priority is opening doors to new ways of thinking about how settlements could and should be planned.

Another helpful concept from the Ecocity project is the 'city of short distances' whose overarching common sense offers workable solutions to many of the key challenges. The city of short distances is a valuable guide for a design process predicated on the advantages of compactness and proximity for buildings and spaces as a means of generating the convenient and efficient use of urban space. To do so it ranks all major forms of mobility, putting walking, cycling and public transport at the top, followed by space allocated to commercial vehicles and lastly to the movement and parking of private vehicles, at home and in town.

For us to lead a healthy life we need an environment that enables it. Its aim to prioritise conditions for health and wellbeing explores the benefits to be gained from the seven targets:

1. Clean air
2. Contact with nature
3. Social interaction
4. Feeling safe
5. Living somewhere healthy
6. Peace and tranquillity
7. Regular exercise.

The planning of new settlements or re-planning of existing ones can create the conditions that will serve these goals, and a good starting point is to consider how they can help to overcome avoidable illnesses and contribute to good health.

## CLEAN AIR

Scientific monitoring has revealed that the air quality in large areas of our city centres exceeds WHO standards and has been leading to increased incidence of respiratory illnesses and dementia. 'Lethal and illegal: London's air pollution crisis' provides evidence that 'Approximately 50% of air pollution comes from road transport and 40% comes from diesel.'[2]

Particulate matter type PM2.5 also contributes to the pollutants and are toxic hazards caused not only by fossil fuel vehicles but also by the brakes and tyres of electric vehicles initially regarded as the obvious, hazard-free solution to address $CO_2$ emissions in town centres. This is a drawback that is routinely overlooked and requires awareness to be raised.

Manufacturing industries can be a further cause of pollution but, provided the risks are minimised and understood in advance, these can be located on sites far enough from key receptors to avoid causing harm. But heating, ventilation and air-conditioning systems of commercial and residential buildings can also be sources of pollutants that are detrimental to air quality.

Public spaces, homes and schools must be protected by zero-tolerance regulations regarding air quality to agree safe locations that will avoid air pollutants exceeding health limits. The statistic for London revealing that '24.6% of all educational establishments are in areas that breach the legal limit for $NO_2$', is an alarming example that shows the seriousness of the threats to public health caused by poor air quality.[3]

To aid air quality, private vehicles must be electric, and they must adhere to the 10-15 mph speed limits of 'Home Zones' to minimise the toxic emissions of particulate matter from brakes, tyres and road surfaces. These low speeds also reduce the likelihood and severity of traffic accidents.

Addressing the threats caused by poor air quality is a matter of urgency, as it affects all who spend time in the public realm and can have lasting impacts on public health. The primary health benefit of clean air will be a decrease in respiratory illnesses, asthma and dementia by limiting motorised traffic, but this in itself generates other health benefits. Controls on traffic will increase the numbers of us adapting to active travel, and this can offset some of the problems of the obesity caused by sedentary lifestyles by integrating exercise into daily life.

The changes in traffic management to be friendlier for pedestrians will increase the attractiveness of the public realm, making it a more desirable place to visit and increasing the likelihood of chance or planned social interaction. This can lead to the psychological benefits of feeling part of a community and making our lives more interesting and enjoyable, and can also be of help to people suffering from feelings of loneliness and isolation.

## CONTACT WITH NATURE

When green spaces are referred to as the lungs of a city the focus is naturally drawn to air quality. Whilst clean air does indeed contribute to our respiratory health, there are additional benefits to be gained from taking exercise outdoors that include social interaction enjoyed in a relaxed environment, the beauty and interest of the greenery and biodiversity in nature and our awareness of watching how the seasons change. The positive psychological benefits of green spaces are particularly important for people whose homes may not offer enough quiet or refuge.

Neuroscientific studies in Denmark and Germany have shown we respond positively to greenery, caused by impulses in the brain's cortex and amygdala. Contact with greenery and spending time outdoors is invaluable not only because of the contributions it makes to mental health and wellbeing but also in treating several forms of cancer, whilst the outdoor exercise it offers helps to reduce respiratory illnesses and incidence of cardiovascular diseases and type 2 diabetes. The medical profession has been in favour of incorporating greenery in the design of hospitals, stating that 'There is currently an increasing (and convincing) evidence base to show that exposure to the natural environment positively affects physical health and mental wellbeing.'[4]

The benefits of green space extend to the moderating influence it has on natural forces. The absorbency of green spaces attenuates runoff from storm water, assisted by the capacity of foliage to retain rainwater droplets. Trees reduce wind-speeds and make a major contribution to limiting the effects of urban heat islands caused by the combination of the fabric and emissions of buildings and overuse of impermeable hard landscaping.

Greenery and water must be integrated into a settlement's structure to make them accessible on foot from homes and workplaces in 5 to 10 minutes. Their size can range from that of intimate pocket parks up to the expansive public facilities able to accommodate large numbers of people. Having an allotment combines several physical and mental health benefits at once: time spent in green space, exercise outdoors, social interaction, nurturing plants and having healthy food to eat and flowers to enjoy.

## SOCIAL INTERACTION

Communication builds community and generates a sense of belonging that helps us feel connected to the places where we live and work, so our settlements need to have a sense of civic pride and an identity to which we can relate. The Centre for Active Design's document 'Assembly: Civic Design Guidelines' reports that 'design can create an important foundation for improving local democracy and opening the lines of communication between citizens and local government'.[5] The location and character of key streets, spaces and buildings determine the attractiveness of the public realm where social interaction takes place. Design strategies employed to create destinations that offer a broad mix of uses that are easy to access and fun to explore are ideal places to greet existing acquaintances and get to know new ones. Social diversity and inclusivity must underpin the designs of these spaces, and high quality outcomes are most likely to be achieved when the community has been involved in a collaborative process of shaping it. 'Assembly's research explores opportunities to leverage design to foster local democracy, reduce civic inequalities, and help all community members feel informed and empowered'.[6]

Social interaction is central to our mental health, providing us with stimulation and the opportunity to exchange information with people we meet and playing an important role in maintaining our sense of belonging to a community. It is equally important for its potential to ameliorate suffering from the loneliness and isolation that can affect people of all ages but is of particular concern amongst older people who can find it hard to keep pace with the explosion of digital technologies. The design of residential accommodation and its spatial connections to areas of lively public realm must combine easy access to shopping and social facilities that offer interesting experiences such as public art installations and events to capture the imagination. Engaging in such activities in the local area is also likely to offer the important benefits of exercise in daily life.

## FEELING SAFE

Fear of crime can be a disincentive to social interaction by causing anxiety about venturing out from the safety of home. Fear of crime as opposed to the likelihood of experiencing its actual risks involves a complex mix of emotions regarding personal and collective safety. It can have undesirable effects by making the public realm less sociable and generating a vicious circle that can lead to increased fear, loneliness and isolation, and higher levels of crime.

Good architectural and urban design have key roles to play in creating places with the qualities to minimise and hopefully overcome these risks. It requires a legible system of streets and spaces addressed by housing designed so as to avoid possible ambiguity between public and private spaces. Neighbourhoods should be arranged to encourage sociability, be overlooked by 'eyes on the street' and served by well-planned street-lighting on traffic-calmed streets, designed for pedestrian priority and with a 20 mph speed limit.

'Secured by Design' is a well known system included in 'Police Crime Prevention Initiatives' (PCPI), that has been developed by the UK police force to minimise crime and anti-social behaviour and performs an essential role as a consultee for urban design and planning.[7] The targeted advice available through PCPIs needs to be accompanied by the broader aspects of governance provided by local authorities and the local initiatives taken by organisations such as 'Neighbourhood Watch' and residents' associations.

People of all ages and walks of life can suffer from fear of crime, and levels of vulnerability can relate to complex matters such as age, gender and ethnicity. Child-friendliness in design is important in enabling young people to benefit from greater independence when accessing facilities in their neighbourhood and the wider urban environment; and for parents to feel that any associated risks are manageable. Ghent in Belgium is one of several European cities that have been pioneering the development of child and youth-friendly policies, part of its action plan being to involve children and youngsters in the creation of 'a new path towards a friendly city'.[8]

In places where a high level of safety has been established, the confidence and reduced sense of isolation created within the community has psychological benefits which will then boost physical health; a result of citizens' increased willingness to make use of active travel in order to spend time in the public realm.

## LIVING SOMEWHERE HEALTHY

The healthiness of the materials, construction and interiors of residential accommodation is a study in itself, but the location and distribution of dwellings are central to healthy placemaking. Homes must avoid car dependency by being at a residential density that, without being over-developed, is high enough to support regular and dependable public transport services. All dwellings must be within walkable distance of transport stops.

Facilities serving daily needs including affordable, healthy food and places to socialise must be within 10 minutes' walk to make it unnecessary to access them by car. Comfortable access on foot to suitable food stores avoids the problems of 'food deserts' and can be augmented by opportunities for citizens to grow their own produce, fresh-to-eat from their gardens, terraces or allotments. With these in place, healthy life choices become more of a feasible and attractive option.

Primary school facilities must also be easily accessible on foot to provide daily exercise and outdoor experiences for children and parents, and avoid the risks associated with poor air quality caused by toxic emissions at school drop-off areas. Secondary school facilities may be further afield but must be accessible by public transport and served by safe bicycle routes. To minimise health inequalities, health facilities must also be easily accessible by public transport.

The layout of dwellings must offer both privacy and neighbourliness and incorporate social spaces for young and old. By fulfilling these objectives the residents will have the opportunity to reduce the chances of contracting avoidable illnesses and benefit instead from the primary health criteria: clean air to avoid respiratory illnesses, social interaction to build community and avoid loneliness and isolation, healthy eating and exercise in daily life to limit obesity and the likelihood of cardiovascular illnesses, type 2 diabetes and cancers as well as a low risk of vehicle accidents.

## PEACE AND TRANQUILLITY

To live in comfort, we need environments to which we can retreat, giving us time and space for reflection, meditation, worship and other forms of self-healing. Fabijana Popovic, of consultancy Sustania, puts this in perspective: 'The rapid urbanization puts pressure on city planners, policy makers and architects to create healthy, sustainable and socially-functioning cities for the 6.3 billions who will have moved to a city by 2050. One thing is creating homes for all these people, it's another thing to create the spaces between the homes that encourage us to live healthy lives.'[9]

Increasingly sophisticated technologies enable us to carry out with ease tasks that previously would have taken far longer to complete. But an insidious effect of this increased speed is that it accelerates the pace of our lives, and this can lead to undesirable impacts on our health unless we find ways to slow it down. Life can impose many pressures from which we need a break, and relaxation is a necessity, not a luxury. But neuroscientific research has revealed that the relaxation and rest we need can itself be endangered by noise pollution and light pollution, thereby hindering our ability to function. Persistent sources of discomfort from noise pollution can cause stress that gives rise to physiological responses, whether from road traffic, railways, airports or industry.[10, 11] Light pollution can disrupt the molecular clock of our circadian rhythms, which has the potential to wreak havoc on our physical and mental health, affecting the production of melatonin, which regulates sleep, and causing changes in organ and metabolic function.[12]

Mental unrest can have damaging effects on our peace of mind. A relatively recent condition in terms of the need to relax is the previously mentioned 'eco-anxiety' as reported by the Wellcome Trust in its report 'How to cure the eco-anxious': '… those directly affected by a climate change-influenced disaster risk losing homes, livelihoods, and loved ones. Also psychologically distressing are constant uncertainty, worry and stress linked to the possibility of a natural disaster.'[13] The report suggests that, instead of focusing on negative emotions, the effects of eco-anxiety can be ameliorated by taking action, as it offers a greater sense of personal control, and doing so with others shares the weight of emotional burden.

If noise pollution, light pollution or other disruptive impacts cannot be prevented due to the location of dwellings too close to established sources, the recent neuroscientific research on the previously unknown effects can be presented to make the case for professional help and support. This would aim to overcome the threats to the relaxation that is so important for our health and wellbeing, and the new research must also be mobilised at the earliest stage of feasibility studies to ensure that disruptive, environmental health risks are avoided in the planning of all new settlements.

## REGULAR EXERCISE

Leading a sedentary lifestyle increases the likelihood of contracting avoidable, non-communicable diseases (NCDs) and *The Lancet* has also reported that too much sitting, rather than lack of physical exercise, is itself associated with type 2 diabetes, cardiovascular disease, some cancers, and all-cause mortality. This indicates that simply getting off the sofa or office chair on a regular basis is something to take seriously because of the contributions it can make towards long-term health and wellbeing.[14]

But, as well as taking breaks from too much continuous sitting, getting regular, more sustained exercise plays an essential part in avoiding NCDs. Those motivated to take exercise in a gym have a head start but, if the gym lacks appeal, getting exercise in daily life is a simple, cheap and more holistic solution. When regular necessities such as shops and primary schools are within easy access, it encourages walking as the natural thing to do.

If the walking routes are safe, attractive, healthy and designed to encourage social interaction, the overall experience is likely to be enjoyable and to be a source of wellbeing. Speaking in David Israelson's 'Special to The Globe and Mail', Glenn Miller, vice president of education and research for the Canadian Urban Institute commented 'People don't want to walk where there's nothing to look at.'[15]

Access to green spaces is also important to encourage those who prefer to spend time outdoors. This is an ideal choice that is complemented by the additional health benefits of breathing fresh air, enjoying the sun or shade and experiencing contact with the natural world. Greenery can also improve the environment in the form of street trees which soften the street scene, may absorb pollution, slow down wind speeds, create shade and reduce heat island effects.

The reputation of roads as places of noise, pollution and danger is a consequence of the all too common presumption that they are the domain of motor vehicles, a reputation reinforced by drivers exceeding speed limits, and, more recently, the broadcasting of the dangers of toxic emissions. Perceptions are changing, and we are recognising streets and roads as part of the public realm that should be safe, healthy places that all of us have an equal right to use. Along with the increasing urbanisation of our settlements, reduction of vehicle use in towns and cities is being offset by the take-up of the many forms of active travel, including the use of public transport, cycling, walking, scooters and the health benefits of exercise these offer.

Street trees make the urban environment attractive as a place for walking, jogging or socialising, and as measures to minimise pollution and reduce the dominance of moving and parked vehicles, trees make a further contribution to transforming the reputation of these essential urban arteries from one of risk to one of pleasure.

The quest to get the exercise we need applies to all stages of our lives. So it makes sense for walking or cycling to be a daily habit because of the additional advantages it offers of fresh air, contact with nature and social interaction as these also guard against respiratory illnesses, cancers, mental illnesses, loneliness and social isolation, and the reduced likelihood of accidents caused by motor vehicles.

## SUMMARY

The response to the seven health targets can be summarised as:

- campaigning for clean air in our settlements
- having easy access to green spaces, and making use of them
- experiencing the stability and warmth of social interaction in a supportive community
- feeling safe and avoiding fear of crime in the urban environment
- benefitting from a walkable, mixed-use urban structure for convenience in daily life
- having the opportunity to benefit from time spent in quiet and peaceful environments
- avoidance of problems associated with sedentary lifestyles through regular exercise.

This analysis contains considerable overlap within the seven health targets listed above as strategies to help us lead healthy lives. This is because the guidance offered by the targets either addresses several health advantages directly, or has indirect consequences that mean the primary advantage leads to others.

Similarly, the range of avoidable illnesses may be caused by more than one of the unhealthy lifestyle habits that need to be discouraged. Table 2.1 shows the relationship between the seven targets and the health risks they can address, including those whose impacts are either primary or secondary, and it also summarises the key aspects of urban planning that relate to each of the targets.

The seven health targets reinforce one another, offering remedies for the same list of avoidable illnesses, but doing so from different starting points, taking the stance that promotion of health and the avoidance of illness are closely interrelated. Consistency across these two approaches shows them to be mutually compatible; a combination of causes and effects that can underpin the organisation and design of built environments aimed at improving our health and wellbeing. As well as being mutually beneficial, none of the advantages offered by these targets give rise to undesirable side-effects on physical and mental health and wellbeing, as all their impacts are positive.

| SEVEN HEALTH TARGETS | HEALTH RISKS TO BE ADDRESSED | | | | | | RELEVANT URBAN PLANNING CRITERIA |
|---|---|---|---|---|---|---|---|
| **HEALTH SUPPORTING QUALITIES** | Cardio-vascular diseases and type 2 diabetes | Poor diet and food poverty | Several forms of cancer | Respiratory illnesses | Mental illnesses | Vehicle related accidents | |
| CLEAN AIR | ○ | | ○ | ● | ○ | ○ | Limiting emissions and sufficient distance of receptors from pollutants |
| CONTACT WITH NATURE | ● | ● | ● | ● | ● | | Location of green space relative to homes, the benefits of allotments and environmental protection |
| SOCIAL INTERACTION | ○ | | | | ● | | Attractive design of walkable public realm |
| FEELING SAFE | ○ | | | | ● | ○ | Safe, defensible, sociable space, child-friendliness and low traffic speeds |
| LIVING SOMEWHERE HEALTHY | ● | ● | ● | ● | ○ | ● | Active travel and walkable access to daily needs, including healthy food and primary schools |
| PEACE & TRANQUILLITY | | | | ○ | ● | | Access to peaceful places and distancing from sources of pollution caused by noise and light |
| REGULAR EXCERCISE | ● | | ● | ● | ● | ● | Quality of public spaces, safe walking routes, green spaces and the benefits of environmental protection |

PRIMARY EFFECT ●          SECONDARY EFFECT ○

**TABLE 2.1** Diagram of seven health targets

The purpose of these health targets is to inform and guide decision-making on matters of urban planning when health and wellbeing are treated as the top priorities. The targets describe generic relationships that enable typical urban life to function. Having set out what the targets for health and wellbeing aim to achieve, it is relevant to consider the healthiness of the procurement process by which they will be delivered into the urban or rural context. This is where participation and collaboration have a part to play.

# PARTICIPATORY PLACEMAKING IS HEALTHY

### HEALTHY PROCUREMENT

For a masterplanning project to get underway a design brief is needed and there are different ways this can be formulated. It is worth considering two contrasting approaches for the preparation of a design brief – the competitive and the participatory.

The competitive approach requires a brief that consists of a package of information setting out all aspects of what the project is to entail. Qualified professionals will carry out research and surveys and also take into account the clients' aspirations. The entrants respond to this using their design skills, often ignoring some aspects of the brief.

The outcome will be designs to be judged by a jury panel selected for their qualifications, holding their own opinions and perhaps not regarding the brief as sacrosanct. The winning project may well depart from the brief because its authors could not have foreseen the ideas the entrants would use to make their unique pitch. In some cases, a single compelling idea or image will win the day, despite ignoring key requirements, and the winners are asked to make amendments to the design. Creative design is full of complexity and many great projects have been produced on this basis, so if twists and turns occur in the process it does not mean anything is amiss.

Participatory planning generates its brief not by defining a set of criteria from the outset but by discovering the most important concepts through a process in which the collaborative evolution of ideas plays a

| COMPETITIVE PLANNING – PARTICIPATORY PLANNING<br>ARCHITECT'S VISION – CONSENSUS VISION |
|---|
| **Stage 1 C (3-6 weeks):** Detailed competition brief prepared, based on judgement of small group of appointed individuals<br>**Stage 1 P (3-6 weeks):** Background information assembled by the design team and local authority staff |
| **Stage 2 C (Launch):** Competitors must interpret the guidance in the brief whilst using their creativity to outdo the other participants<br>**Stage 2 P (1 week):** Public or stakeholder Charrette workshop; simultaneous exploration of ideas generates a consensus brief |
| **Stage 3 C (8-16 weeks):** A range of competing submissions, but has the jury understood or respected the brief?<br>**Stage 3 P:** An integrated plan combining the best outcomes of the workshop contributions becomes a consensus vision with a shared sense of ownership |
| **Stage 4 C (1-2 weeks):** The jury's verdict: The hope is that the winner is selected on content rather than a 'beauty parade'<br>**Stage 4 P( 6-13 weeks):** Creative design development continues within the framework of the consensus masterplan |
| **P Plan finalised:** Total period to production of participatory masterplan – 10-20 weeks |
| **Stage 5 C (6-13 weeks):** The design often requires re-working to be deliverable<br>**Stage 5 P:** The masterplan can either be developed by the existing team, divided into separate parcels for detailed architectural competitions or shared out amongst development companies |
| **C Plan finalised:** Total period to production of competitive masterplan – 18-37 weeks |

**TABLE 2.2**
Competitive planning and participatory planning schematic schedules

pivotal part in determining the project's future. Instead of a written brief the organisers prepare comprehensive background information in advance about the site's technical strengths and weaknesses, to inform an intense brainstorming event to which the public is invited. Details of how this process is managed are described in Chapter 3.6, but the main thrust is that a consensus brief of key themes emerges through the workshop process, from which collaboratively-designed sketch proposals are generated to arrive at a shared vision. The design is by no means fixed but the community's involvement leads to a sense of ownership and a robust direction of travel with the flexibility to accommodate changes as the project moves forward.

Whilst the competitive brief generates a broad range of unique concepts from which one is selected, the participatory approach uses collective energy step by step to establish a shared belief in how the site should be developed. The case study for Berliner Platz, Essen, Germany in Chapter 3.4, describes how that particular project evolved through a classic, participatory process selected in preference to the initial intention to hold an open competition.

The preceding table is a schematic schedule, using the letter 'C' for Competitive and 'P' for Participatory, showing the different activities taking place during successive stages of the project. The participatory approach is intrinsically faster due to the intensity and speed of the brainstorming process.

## HEALTHY PARTICIPATION

As illustrated in the previous section on 'Cities growing healthily', social interaction and building community are central to healthy placemaking. This can be seen when witnessing the strength of feeling amongst local communities where changes are proposed that will disrupt the pattern of the existing urban structure. The development teams need to recognise that they are merely short-term visitors to a place that has a history perhaps freighted with meaning for people whose home it has been for decades, if not longer. A significant element behind this strength of feeling is the knowledge local people have amassed about the changes the place has undergone over the years, for better or for worse.

It is obvious that existing communities deserve respect both as local residents and as local experts, and it makes sense for them to be involved early in the design process, as their collective knowledge of the past and present means they should also be involved in shaping its future.

The final section of Chapter 1, *Healthy Planet*, concludes with Dr Frumkin's statement that 'Humans can't be healthy on a planet that isn't healthy'.[16] This connects with the idea that places can only be healthy if they are the result of a healthy procurement process, as the healthiness of a place resides as much in the contentment it generates amongst the local community as in the shape of its built form and spatial organisation.

Architectural and planning projects create places, buildings and spaces that have a fundamental impact on people's lives and, once constructed, are likely to remain as a fixture far into the future. As construction is costly, complex and risky, the process tends to be dominated by professional organisations with the resources to invest in them. Local authorities consult their local communities to ensure that design proposals are publicly accessible, but consultation is not the same as participation. When consultation is treated by the development industry as a necessary obstacle to the granting of planning permission and getting on with the job, local groups are likely to feel marginalised and powerless, yet it is they who will not only have to live with whatever is built in their neighbourhood but must also put up with disruption during the construction process. An alternative approach is for development companies to involve the local community at an early stage, creating an atmosphere that is collaborative rather than adversarial and likely to offer benefits to all concerned.

It will still be a negotiation but regular communication about what is planned can clear the air and overcome misunderstandings. The community can contribute its local knowledge and experience of the neighbourhood by flagging-up important information that benefits the proposed design.

Inviting local people to play a part in decision-making shows they are respected and valued. Social networks are expanded as understanding grows about the constraints, opportunities, consensus points and dilemmas that shape the design proposals as they evolve. This in turn can generate a shared feeling of ownership for the project and a sense of purpose from having been involved.

The collaborative nature of this approach is what makes it a healthy design process that can strengthen the cohesiveness of communities. The ability to function within an interconnected society improves the social fabric, enhances sociability and inspires confidence for residents and stakeholders. Harnessing local knowledge to help design environments that fulfil people's needs and aspirations is of immense value, and an effective way of doing so is through collaborative working processes such as 'Community Planning'.

It is a highly creative process to be employed at the early, conceptual stage as a means of establishing the most desirable overall direction for the project. Its most desirable output is a compelling and memorable vision that encapsulates the most important ideas that are retained as guidance for subsequent phases. This type of experience adds meaning and a sense of belonging that is one of the cornerstones for health, an idea developed further in Chapter 3.6 on *Community Empowerment*.

## CHAPTER 3

# FROM THEORY TO PRACTICE

*'The benefits of designing streets around pedestrians and cyclists and reducing car use can be enjoyed by everyone and will help ensure the future of our high streets.'*[1]

**WILL NORMAN**

# INTRODUCTION

This chapter introduces the six principles of healthy placemaking that can be applied in practice to create places that are beneficial for our long-term health. Each principle has a rationale behind it supported by case studies and best practice examples. These can instil confidence in the reader that change for the better is possible and that it has been implemented successfully in many places.

The preceding chapters summarise how the environments that have developed over time, and the lifestyles they serve, have had impacts on the health and wellbeing of individuals and communities. The challenge people now face is how to combine enjoying a good quality of life with steering clear of the risks of avoidable illnesses. This can be influenced by the way places are planned, based on the six principles of healthy placemaking.

Chapter 2 presented a set of strategies whose interrelated qualities can contribute to the creation of health-supporting environments in which to live. These strategies are not intended to guide the design of layouts for actual sites. Instead, the topics they cover are incorporated within the broader scope of text and diagrams that lead from theory to practice.

# SIX PRINCIPLES
# FOR HEALTHY PLACEMAKING

The six principles for healthy placemaking form the overall framework for the book, consisting of high-level topics relating to the issues and ideas covered. The titles of principles one to five indicate that they address different aspects of spatial organisation, whilst the focus of principle six emphasises the role that social interaction plays as the foundation of community empowerment.

The six principles of healthy placemaking are:

1. Urban planning.
2. Walkable communities.
3. Neighbourhood building blocks.
4. Movement networks.

**5.** Environmental integration.

**6.** Community empowerment.

**1. URBAN PLANNING –** an overall structure consisting of a series of connected neighbourhoods united as communities.

- Active travel is limited when dispersed uses lead to car dependency.
- Compact, mixed-use urban structures allow shorter travel distances and easier mobility.
- This leads to reduced congestion, better air quality and healthier lifestyles.

**2. WALKABLE COMMUNITIES –** a compact, centrally-located heart, close enough to be accessible to all by foot or bicycle, benefitting from social interaction within an attractive and lively public realm.

- Motor vehicles, whether in motion or parked, take up too much space in towns.
- We walk or cycle when our daily needs are easy to reach, benefitting from the exercise and saving time.
- A lively, attractive public realm is stimulating and promotes social interaction.

**3. NEIGHBOURHOOD BUILDING BLOCKS –** a series of focus points consisting of housing and mixed-uses where locals with interests in common can meet on a social basis, learn and share new skills and develop local businesses.

- Poor living conditions and social isolation diminish the quality of our lives.
- Well-designed, well-managed buildings and public spaces generate a sense of security and ownership in local communities.
- The combination of mixed-uses and dwellings creates local focus and reference points for adjacent neighbourhoods.

**4. MOVEMENT NETWORKS –** active travel mandatory within walkable communities, other than residents' access allowed for clean vehicles only and deliveries at controlled times. Parking for vehicles arriving on larger roads only permitted at the periphery of walkable communities.

- People in cars tend to think that traffic is caused by other people.

- Providing many options for sustainable 'active travel' makes getting about safer; breathing cleaner air.
- Vehicle accidents under 20 mph are unlikely to cause fatalities. The '20's Plenty!' concept is desirable for mixed-use streets.

**5. ENVIRONMENTAL INTEGRATION –** green/blue spaces weaving through the urban structure and being accessible from all dwellings within less than 10 minutes' walk.

- Time spent in green space is good for our physical and mental health.
- Parks, play facilities, gardens and allotments are places that improve the quality of our lives and help to build communities.
- Trees and shrubs contribute to comfortable microclimates and biodiversity; a natural protection from flooding, strong winds and overheating.

**6. COMMUNITY EMPOWERMENT –** encouragement for groups to meet, exchange ideas and promote initiatives both within each Walkable Community and by connecting with neighbouring ones.

- Communities become emotionally attached to the design of their neighbourhoods, enhancing their quality of life.
- Our imagination is captured when we work with our neighbours to improve the places where we live.
- This sense of collaboration is a potent force that strengthens social networks, raises aspirations and leads to positive change.

These six principles can be subdivided further into two groups; three scales of planning and three linking concepts.

In response to their differing scales, urban planning, walkable communities and neighbourhood building blocks are served by the influences of movement networks, environmental integration and community empowerment. And the linking concepts of the latter three each need to adapt, to address the requirements of urban planning, walkable communities and neighbourhood building blocks.

The interweaving of the grid diagram produces a different block of colour for each of the nine intersections to reinforce the message that all of the six principles relate to one another. This emphasises that the benefits each principle may deliver individually is secondary to the impacts generated through the combined effect of them all. Connection and integration are fundamental to the ethos of healthy placemaking.

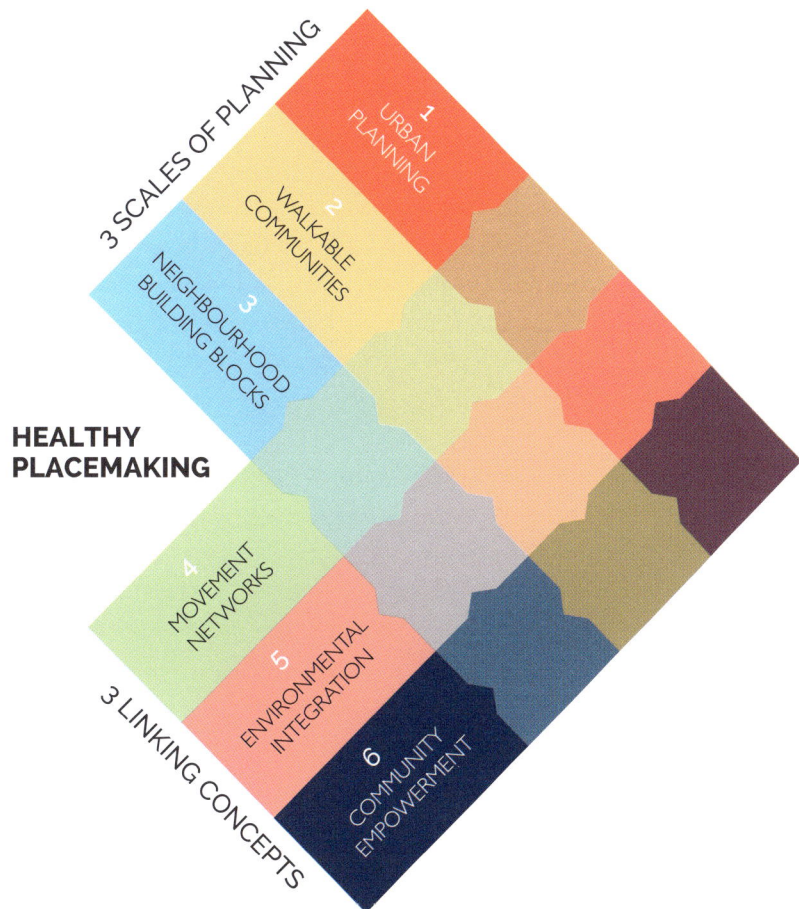

3 SCALES OF PLANNING

1 URBAN PLANNING

2 WALKABLE COMMUNITIES

3 NEIGHBOURHOOD BUILDING BLOCKS

**HEALTHY PLACEMAKING**

4 MOVEMENT NETWORKS

5 ENVIRONMENTAL INTEGRATION

6 COMMUNITY EMPOWERMENT

3 LINKING CONCEPTS

**FIGURE 3.0.1**
Healthy Placemaking
Interweaving diagram - the
ethos of healthy placemaking

# HEALTH CHART

The range of topics covered by the six principles and the avoidable illnesses to which they relate make it hard to assess their relative importance, as some effects are generic whilst others are more specific. The Health Chart diagram, Table 3.0.1, illustrates this in the form of a table using a simple scoring system. The table indicates how the bullet points under each principle perform with regard to the environmental and social measures that can be taken in response to the causes of the illnesses.

Table 1.1 (Chapter 1) sets out the main health problems, their causes and how to address them. The Health Chart diagram makes use of Table 1.1 to 'test' the six healthy placemaking principles and associated bullet points against those health problems, in order to provide an overview of the areas where each bullet point can contribute health benefits.

This reveals the significant variation between how the bullet points measure up against the health problems. The scores are subjective but serve as reference points for comparison with a further diagram in the sub-section on 'Generic Methodology' that follows, which expands on the Health Chart concept.

The easiest way to summarise the Health Chart diagram is to follow the downward columns from the headings in line with 'addressing the causes':

- 'Enable exercise in daily life', for instance, is well represented under the principles of urban planning, walkable communities, movement networks and environmental integration.
- 'Provision of education, accessible facilities and available green space', which address the same health problems as 'exercise in daily life', the focus comes under environmental integration and community empowerment.
- 'Limiting the causes and effects of vehicular emissions' is mainly represented under urban planning, movement networks and environmental integration.
- 'Community facilities and safe, sociable, productive environments' figure strongly under all six principles.

**TABLE 3.0.1** (Page 49)
Health Chart diagram

| MAIN HEALTH PROBLEMS | Cardiovascular disease, type 2 diabetes, and obesity; several forms of cancer (referred to as 'avoidable illnesses') | Respiratory diseases including asthma | Poor air quality | Mental illnesses | Transport related accidents | FREQUENCY |
|---|---|---|---|---|---|---|
| CAUSES | Sedentary lifestyles and lack of excercise | Poor diet and food poverty | Poor air quality | Loneliness, isolation, limited social interaction and fear of crime | Impacts of vehicles and interaction with cycles and pedestrians | |
| ADDRESSING THE CAUSES | Enable excercise in daily life | Provide education, accessible facilities and available green spaces | Limit the effects of vehicular emissions | Community facilities and safe, sociable, productive environments | Good urban and transport design | |
| **URBAN PLANNING** — Active travel is limited when dispersed uses lead to car-dependency | | | | | | |
| Compact mixed use urban structures allow shorter travel distances and easier mobility | 2 | | 2 | 1 | 2 | 7 |
| This leads to reduced congestion, better air quality and healthier lifestyles | 2 | | 2 | 1 | 1 | 6 |
| Inclusive, vibrant neighbourhoods generate a sense of community and wellbeing | 2 | 2 | 2 | 2 | | 8 |
| | | | | | | 21 |
| **WALKABLE COMMUNITIES** — Motor vehicles, whether in motion or parked, take up too much space in towns | | | | | | |
| We walk or cycle when our daily needs are easy to reach, benefitting from the exercise and saving time | 2 | | 2 | 2 | 1 | 7 |
| A lively, attractive public realm is stimulating and promotes social interaction | 2 | | | 2 | 1 | 5 |
| Health-supporting amenities like fresh food, healthcare and leisure facilities should also be nearby | 1 | 2 | | 2 | | 5 |
| | | | | | | 17 |
| **NEIGHBOURHOOD BUILDING BLOCKS** — Poor living conditions and social isolation diminish the quality of our lives | | | | | | |
| Well-designed, well-managed buildings and public spaces generate a sense of security and ownership in the local community | | | | 2 | 1 | 3 |
| The combination of mixed uses and dwellings creates a local focus and reference point for adjacent neighbourhoods | 2 | 1 | | 2 | 1 | 6 |
| | | | | | | 9 |
| **MOVEMENT NETWORKS** — People in cars tend to think that traffic is caused by other people | | | | | | |
| Taking advantage of the many options for sustainable 'active travel' makes getting about safer and breathing cleaner air | 2 | | 2 | 2 | 2 | 8 |
| Vehicle accidents under 20 mph are unlikely to cause fatalities. The '20's Plenty!' concept is desirable for mixed-use streets | 2 | | 1 | 1 | 2 | 6 |
| | | | | | | 14 |
| **ENVIRONMENTAL INTEGRATION** — Time spent in green space is good for our physical and mental health | | | | | | |
| Parks, play facilities, gardens and allotments are places that improve the quality of our lives and help to build communities | 2 | 2 | 2 | 2 | | 8 |
| Trees and shrubs contribute to comfortable microclimates and biodiversity; a natural protection from flooding and strong winds | 2 | 1 | 2 | 2 | | 7 |
| | | | | | | 15 |
| **COMMUNITY EMPOWERMENT** — Communities become emotionally attached to the design of their neighbourhoods, enhancing their quality of life | | | | | | |
| Our imagination is captured when we work with our neighbours to improve the places where we live | | 1 | 1 | 2 | 1 | 5 |
| This sense of collaboration is a potent force that strengthens social networks, raises aspirations and leads to positive change | | 2 | 1 | 2 | 1 | 6 |
| | | | | | | 11 |
| Scoring: 0=Not relevant  1=Potentially relevant  2=Significantly relevant  **Total** | 21 | 11 | 17 | 25 | 13 | 87 |

- 'Good urban and transport design' is concentrated under urban planning and movement networks but with a wider spread at lower level in walkable communities, neighbourhood building blocks and community empowerment.

The Health Chart does not rank these issues according to their seriousness or implications on health, but shows the pattern of the ways the health problems can be addressed by the six healthy placemaking principles.

# CONCEPTUAL DIAGRAMS

A conceptual diagram representing the six principles for healthy placemaking is illustrated by a series of bold icons that are combined to create the basic, spatial organisation of a single walkable community. A second diagram adapts this pattern to show how three of these walkable communities could be combined to make a larger settlement; an approach that can be replicated further for yet larger settlements.

The individual diagram, Figure 3.0.2, shows a single walkable community with a centrally-located, mixed-use and residential heart, with shops and social facilities that are accessible on foot within 10 minutes from the settlement's periphery. Residential neighbourhoods at a variety of densities are set within an inter-connected network of green/blue spaces, and the housing areas are punctuated by the smaller-scale focal points of neighbourhood building blocks.

Vehicular access into the walkable community is limited to residents, is emission-free, pedestrian-priority, traffic-calmed and also permits clean modes of public transport to serve the mixed-use heart. Deliveries are allowed at agreed times of day only, and emergency services can access required destinations as necessary. The red-dotted arrows represent community empowerment that is shown focusing on the mixed-use heart but would also relate to the neighbourhood building blocks and permeate the whole community. The limitations on vehicular traffic and parking mean that the walkable community will be compact and safe, thereby facilitating social interaction and promoting a sense of belonging.

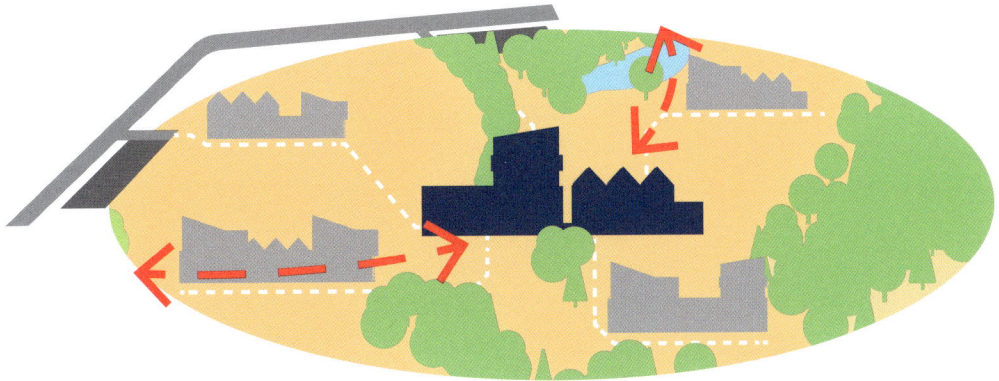

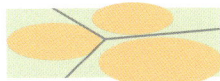

URBAN
PLANNING

WALKABLE
COMMUNITIES

NEIGHBOURHOOD
BUILDING BLOCKS

MOVEMENT
NETWORKS

ENVIRONMENTAL
INTEGRATION

COMMUNITY
EMPOWERMENT

**FIGURE 3.0.2**
Integrated Concept
– individual

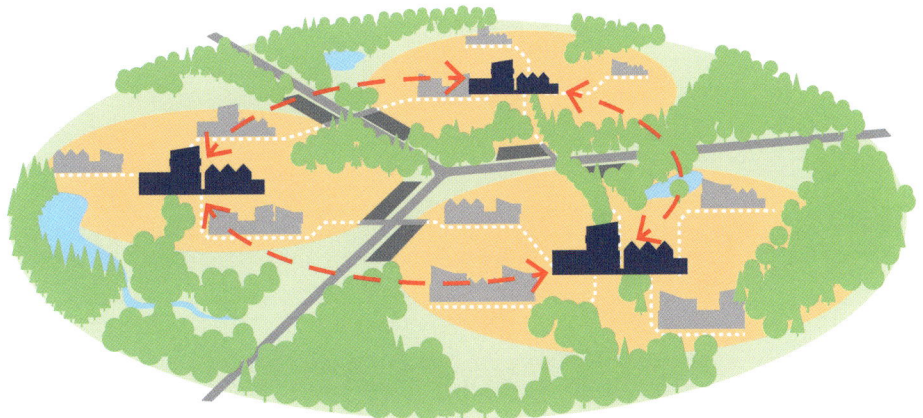

**FIGURE 3.0.3**
Integrated Concept
– three combined

The routes of public roads run along the edge of each walkable community where vehicles arriving from external destinations can make use of parking facilities immediately adjacent to the roads. This means that businesses dependent on vehicular access for their own needs and those of customers must also be located adjacent to the road system to avoid unwanted commercial traffic entering the interior of the walkable community.

Figure 3.0.3, the diagram that combines three walkable communities, indicates the many ways they are united. It shows the road system shared to serve all three whilst each community retains its individual identity. Together, these three communities share the interconnected green/blue infrastructure and the potential for community empowerment and neighbourhood building blocks to form broader interest-groups.

Although illustrated as a new settlement, the principles are equally applicable to the adaptation of existing places.

## AREAS AND DENSITIES

Although these diagrams are conceptual and devoid of measurable dimensions they are nonetheless based on a clear rationale of land use that allows developable areas and population to be estimated at a range of possible densities. The overall area of one walkable community has been chosen as 200 hectares because this has a radius of 800 m, amounting to a 10-minute walk at 3 mph that matches its designation as a walkable community.

A basic rule of thumb is that residential land use occupies approximately 50% of a site's overall land-take, the other half consisting of public facilities

**TABLE 3.0.2**
Population densities and
residential building typologies

| DENSITY | TYPOLOGIES | APPROXIMATE POPULATION |
|---|---|---|
| Low density | Only houses | 7,000 |
| Medium density | Mixture of houses and apartments | 13,000 |
| Medium-high density | Mostly apartments | 19,000 |

such as schools, health centres and administration, spaces for employment, retail and food outlets, entertainment, green space and other natural features, public squares and public and private transport infrastructure including vehicle parking.

At 50% of the overall site area, the estimated land-take for residential development would be 100 hectares on which the housing itself can be at a wide variety of densities.

Figure 3.0.3 demonstrates how several could be joined together to make a larger settlement. With a balanced mix of all three densities, the population for one neighbourhood would average out at 13,000 and the population of the three together would total 39,000; equivalent to that of a small-/medium-sized town. If all areas were at low density the population would be 21,000 and, if all were at medium-high density, 57,000.

## BUILDINGS, SPACES, ACTIVITIES AND HEALTH

Figure 3.0.4 complements the 'Integrated Concept' diagrams with images of indicative buildings around some public spaces in a walkable community. But its main purpose is to show the inter-relationships between the buildings, spaces and the uses and activities that take place in them, and how they can work together to create healthy environments. It does so in three stages:

1. Describing what takes place in the four types of land use.
2. Explaining the health benefits those activities can offer.
3. Listing the health risks these activities can help people to avoid.

It is an example of connected strategies achievable though the combined effect of the layout of buildings and spaces and the activities that take place in them.

## GENERIC METHODOLOGY

Showing how the health of settlements can be improved makes a valuable contribution to planning submissions. The process that underpins the UK's planning approval system requires the submission of a number of documents to support the planning drawings. A key document is the Design and Access

| FEATURES | MIXED-USE BLOCKS 1 & 2 | PUBLIC SPACE | MOVEMENT SYSTEM | GREEN SPACE |
|---|---|---|---|---|
| **USES & FACILITIES** | Ground floor retail, affordable healthy food and drink, employment, social facilities, mixed-tenure apartments on upper floors. | Active frontage to buildings, market stalls, seating, shelter, greenery, events space, children's play | Prioritised active travel, public transport service, traffic calming, 20mph max, broad pavements, pedestrian priority, shared road space, ultra-low-emission vehicles, street trees, discreetly-located vehicle parking | Trees, water, wildflower meadow, orchard, allotments, biodiversity, eco-information centre and café, outdoor seating, children's play, stormwater attenuation, urban cooling |
| **HEALTH BENEFITS** | Building diverse inclusive community, 'eyes on the street', healthy diet, green balconies, roof gardens | Social interaction in vibrant setting, accessible and local facilities | Clean air, shade from street trees, daily exercise, safe streets | A therepeutic environment, clean air, shade, education, reduced eco-anxiety, healthy diet |
| **HEALTH RISK REDUCTION** | Mental illnesses from social isolation, loneliness, fear of crime, food poverty, health poverty | Mental illnesses from social isolation, loneliness, fear of crime | Respiratory illnesses, cardiovascular diseases, type 2 diabetes, several forms of cancer, transport related accidents | Respiratory illnesses, cardiovascular diseases, type 2 diabetes, several forms of cancer, mental illnesses |

| MIXED-USE BLOCK 1 | PUBLIC SQUARE | MOVEMENT SYSTEM | MIXED-USE BLOCK 2 | GREEN SPACE |

**TABLE 3.0.3**
(Page 54) The health benefits
associated with building
typologies and public spaces

Statement (DAS) whose purpose is to describe all aspects of the project, within which sustainability and healthy placemaking are important topics. The Health Chart, Table 3.0.1, shows how the six healthy placemaking principles relate to avoidable illnesses and the measures that urban planning can offer to address them. The chart is also a reference point for the methodology set out here which expands it for incorporation in the project's DAS. It is to be used for the assessment of the health credentials of design projects, and the methodology consists of two elements; the expanded table (Table 3.0.4) and a plan drawing (Figure 3.0.5) showing the components of the proposed health-enhancing interventions.

The adaptation of the table involves making two versions: one that assesses the healthiness of the existing site before redevelopment and another that compares it with the intended health improvements resulting from the design proposals. This analysis enables architects, urbanists and masterplanners to assess the design's success in improving the healthiness of the project, including consideration of the design's relationship to the context outside the site boundary.

Use of the same set of points for the Health Chart and DAS diagram to carry out the assessment enables design companies to compare the outcomes from project to project. Every project has such a wealth of unique characteristics that the numerical outcome created by the scoring system is not to be treated as a definitive conclusion. Instead the scores are to be used as guidance for descriptive, analytical text that, in conjunction with the drawn plan, summarises the specific circumstances of the project.

To fill in these 'before and after' tables requires the insertion of a brief entry in the box next to each bullet point to explain the extent to which the design proposals meet the criteria, as shown in Table 3.0.4. These statements inform the decisions about the scores, as appropriate, to arrive at the overall numerical rating.

(NB: Table 3.0.4 illustrates the assessment methodology for the design proposals but not that of the existing site. However, the scores for the existing site are shown in the column next to those of the proposals, making comparison easy and, as stated above, the actual assessment is in the form of a written description plus the plan drawing, not the numbers.

**FIGURE 3.0.4**
(Page 54) Building typologies
and public spaces

| | | Main Health Problems | Cardiovascular disease, type 2 diabetes, and obesity; several forms of cancer (referred to as 'avoidable illnesses') | Respiratory diseases including asthma | Mental illnesses | Transport related accidents | | |
|---|---|---|---|---|---|---|---|---|
| **Detailed Planning Application for 200 dwelling residential development within wider area Outline Planning Application** | **Design Proposals** | **Causes** | Obesity caused by sedentary lifestyles and lack of exercise | Poor diet and food poverty | Poor air quality | Loneliness, isolation, limited social interaction and fear of crime | Impacts of vehicles and interaction with cycles and pedestrians | |
| | *To what extent do the Design Proposals meet these Healthy Placemaking principles?* | **Addressing the Causes** | Enable exercise in daily life | Provide education, accessible facilities and available green spaces | Limit the causes and effects of vehicular emissions | Community facilities and safe, sociable, productive environments | Good urban and transport design | Existing site / Proposals |

**UK South Coast small town** — Regeneration of a former military base to form an employment-led mixed use masterplan.

| Principle | Design proposal notes | C1 | C2 | C3 | C4 | C5 | Existing site | Proposals |
|---|---|---|---|---|---|---|---|---|
| **URBAN PLANNING** — *Active travel is limited when dispersed uses lead to car-dependency* | | | | | | | | |
| Compact mixed use urban structures allow shorter travel distances and easier mobility | The outline application is employment-led but provides a mix of uses (light industry/housing commercial) reducing travel distances for many. | 2 | | 1 | 1 | 1 | 0 | 5 |
| This leads to reduced congestion, better air quality and healthier lifestyles | Car use will rise with new occupants but good urban design encourages walking/cycling to nearby amenities, supported by new mixed uses on site. | | | 1 | 1 | 1 | 2 | 5 |
| Inclusive, vibrant neighbourhoods generate a sense of community and wellbeing | New housing will support local demand for small family homes and provide a mix of tenures. Streets and spaces provide an environment for social interaction. | 2 | 1 | 1 | 1 | | 2 | 5 |
| | | | | | | | **4** | **15** |
| **WALKABLE COMMUNITIES** — *Motor vehicles, whether in motion or parked, take up too much space in towns* | | | | | | | | |
| We walk or cycle when our daily needs are easy to reach, benefitting from the exercise and saving time | New connections into existing streets bring the high street within walking distance. Mixed uses in later phases will further reduce travel distances to daily needs. | 2 | | 2 | 2 | 1 | 4 | 7 |
| A lively, attractive public realm is stimulating and promotes social interaction | New footpaths connect to waterfront and neighbouring developments. New public open spaces and enhanced existing historic gardens. New community, 200 homes (c. 500 people). | 1 | | 1 | 2 | 1 | 2 | 5 |
| Health-supporting amenities like fresh food, healthcare and leisure facilities should also be nearby | Access to beachfront and existing high street assets made easier through new connections. 15-20 mins walk to golf course and country park. | 1 | 1 | 1 | 2 | | 3 | 5 |
| | | | | | | | **9** | **17** |
| **NEIGHBOURHOOD BUILDING BLOCKS** — *Poor living conditions and social isolation diminish the quality of our lives* | | | | | | | | |
| Well-designed, well-managed buildings and public spaces generate a sense of security and ownership in the local community | New high quality private and affordable housing. Good overlooking of public spaces. Historic buildings refurbished and re-used, preserving the streetscene. | 1 | | 1 | 2 | 1 | 2 | 5 |
| The combination of mixed uses and dwellings creates a local focus and reference point for adjacent neighbourhoods | New mixed uses are provided for in later phases of outline application. Planned small local shops and offices as well as more new homes and employment areas. | 2 | 1 | | 2 | 1 | 2 | 6 |
| | | | | | | | **4** | **11** |
| **MOVEMENT NETWORKS** — *People in cars tend to think that traffic is caused by other people* | | | | | | | | |
| Taking advantage of the many options for sustainable 'active travel' makes getting about safer and breathing cleaner air | Existing bus along seafront within 400 m, planned re-route through sites. Cycle lanes connect to existing networks. Visitor and cycle parking for homes, on high street and seafront. | 2 | | 1 | 2 | 1 | 4 | 6 |
| Vehicle accidents under 20 mph are unlikely to cause fatalities. The '20's Plenty!' concept is desirable for mixed-use streets | 20 is typically the maximum speed along new residential roads, except Waterfront Drive at 30 which has a separate cycle lane. | 2 | | 1 | 1 | 2 | 4 | 6 |
| | | | | | | | **8** | **12** |
| **ENVIRONMENTAL INTEGRATION** — *Time spent in green space is good for our physical and mental health* | | | | | | | | |
| Parks, play facilities, gardens and allotments are places that improve the quality of our lives and help to build communities | New public open space with integrated play facilities. Green spaces link new homes with existing residential streets via cycle lanes and footpaths. Historic gardens reopened. | 2 | 1 | 2 | 2 | 1 | 4 | 8 |
| Trees and shrubs contribute to comfortable microclimates and biodiversity; a natural protection from flooding and strong winds | Existing trees retained where possible and many new planted. Proximity to beach offers fresh sea air and encourages active lifestyle. | 2 | 1 | 2 | 2 | | 4 | 7 |
| | | | | | | | **8** | **15** |
| **COMMUNITY EMPOWERMENT** — *Communities become emotionally attached to the design of their neighbourhoods, enhancing their quality of life* | | | | | | | | |
| Our imagination is captured when we work with our neighbours to improve the places where we live | Statutory exhibitions were held alongside meetings with local stakeholders and residents' associations. Amendments were made following feedback. | | 2 | | 2 | 1 | 4 | 5 |
| This sense of collaboration is a potent force that strengthens social networks, raises aspirations and leads to positive change | New homes will support the growth of the local community, and further mixed-uses on site in the future should aid integration. | | 2 | | 2 | | 4 | 4 |
| | | | | | | | **8** | **9** |
| Scoring: 0 = not relevant   1 = potentially relevant   2 = significantly relevant | Scoring is used as guidance for written assessment summary | Total 21 | 9 | 14 | 24 | 11 | **41** | **79** |

The project used to explain this methodology is set out below and includes an example of a written assessment.)

## WRITTEN ASSESSMENT

The Healthy Placemaking DAS Plan shown in Figure 3.0.5 is for a project in Lee-on-the-Solent, a relatively low-density, mixed-use neighbourhood in a small UK town. The methodology has also been tested against greenfield sites and high-density, urban projects in the UK, which indicates that its generic system is applicable in widely divergent contexts.

The overall project is for the regeneration of a former military base to form an employment-led mixed-use masterplan, within which a detailed planning application has been submitted for 200 dwellings. These are spread across two sites separated by a swathe of employment facilities and located within an outline planning application for the regeneration of the wider area.

The context surrounding the two sites is disjointed but the insertion of well-planned housing into the two sites, Waterfront West and Waterfront East, can help to consolidate the existing housing stock, provide more legible routes and offer scope for social interaction. New connections will enable easier access on foot to the town centre, with Waterfront East approximately 400 m away and Waterfront West at 750 m.

Both areas of new housing are within 400 m of the existing bus route which, together with the main cycle route, follows the seafront to reach the town centre and goes on to serve the junior and infant and nursery schools which are 1.1 km and 1.4 km away from the new housing. Given these opportunities for active travel, it will be interesting to see how much the bus and cycle routes are used.

The continuous south-west facing seafront is a 10-minute walk from Waterfront East and a few minutes from Waterfront West. The beach and promenade which make it a popular holiday destination provide the new residents with an excellent opportunity for fresh sea air and outdoor exercise. The reopened historic gardens next to Waterfront West contribute to further recreation facilities next to the town centre and the schools and the golf course and country park are a 15- to 20-minute walk to the east.

**TABLE 3.0.4**
(Page 56) Healthy Placemaking DAS diagram, incorporating criteria from the Health Chart, for Lee-on-the-Solent

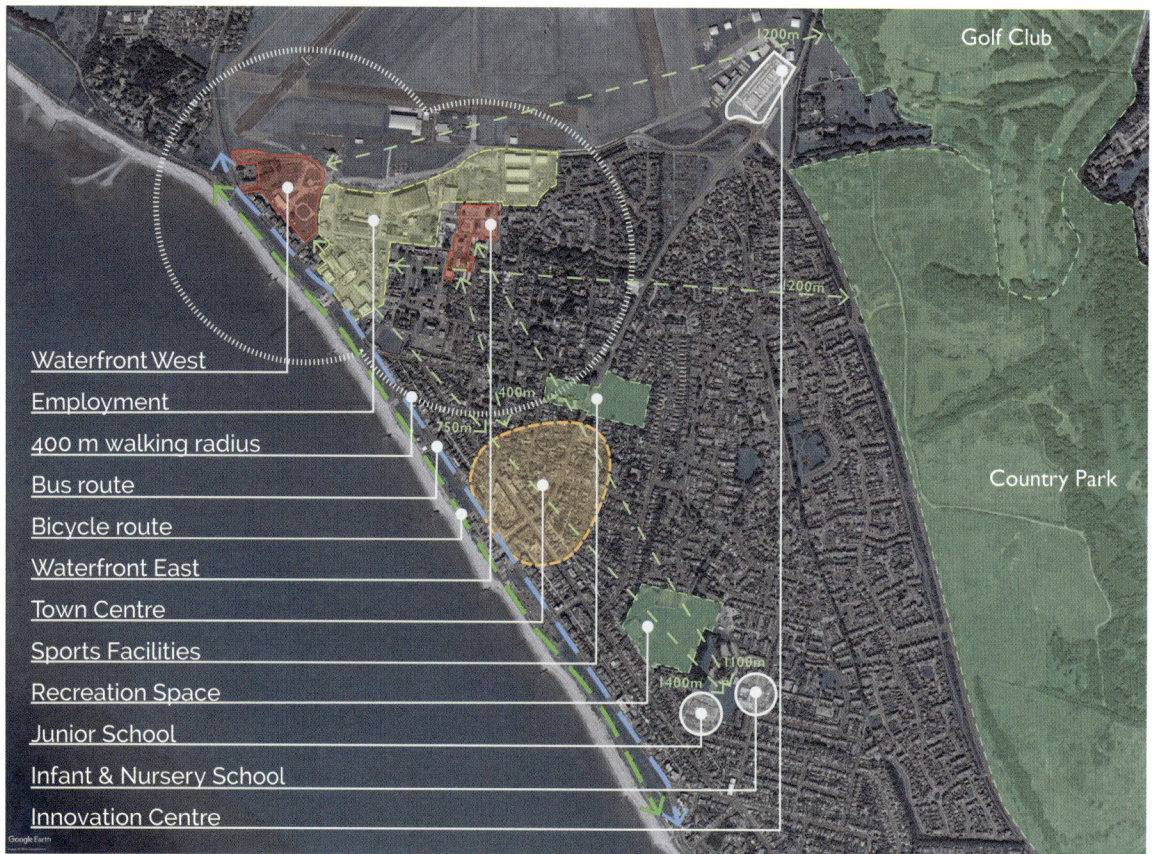

Waterfront West
Employment
400 m walking radius
Bus route
Bicycle route
Waterfront East
Town Centre
Sports Facilities
Recreation Space
Junior School
Infant & Nursery School
Innovation Centre

Golf Club

Country Park

**FIGURE 3.0.5** Healthy Placemaking DAS Plan for Lee-on-the-Solent

The variety of green spaces and the beach provide the town with its healthiest features whilst the level of community engagement is likely to be boosted by the joint influences of the sense of identity regarding the town's military heritage, the arrival of new residents and the overall regeneration process. The current state of disrepair of the two sites is the reason for its proposed regeneration, so the new accommodation will make a significant improvement to its health credentials because of the housing itself and the connections it will contribute to the wider area.

# INDEX OF CASE STUDIES

Amongst the best known, and duly recognised for their overall standards of liveability, are the cities of Freiburg, Copenhagen, Stockholm, Amsterdam, Zürich, Vienna, Melbourne, Singapore and Vancouver. Most or all of these are prosperous, well-managed cities where achieving high standards for quality of life and liveability is attainable. Deeper analysis is required as to the reasons behind their success and whether their qualities could be replicated in other places. For instance, whilst their systems of governance will have created those exceptional outcomes, these may have been instigated as a result of the local community's acceptance of the implications of key decisions.

A good example is Freiburg, Germany, a well-to-do university city where the threat of its energy being provided through the construction of a new nuclear power station caused the population to decide they would prefer to live sustainably, and proceeded to do so. It involved a change of attitude that may not be viewed with the same acceptance and determination in other settlements around the world.

Another example is Zürich, Switzerland where locals understand and accept the rules and significant costs for recycling waste that residents from other countries might well regard as entirely unreasonable. However, outside this elite group are notable examples, including Kenya which has introduced strict rules about plastic bag use; an encouraging sign that awareness of environmental issues is rising in many parts of the world.[2]

All of these exemplar cities recognise areas where they fail to reach the highest standards. This is why the places that have been chosen as case studies were selected to draw attention to specific qualities they demonstrate rather than their overall performance in terms of healthy placemaking. It reminds us that, although nowhere has all the answers, all places have the potential to improve on their weaknesses as much as, if not more than, raising the bar on their strengths.

For ease of reference, the case studies for the following six chapters are:

CHAPTER 3.1
**URBAN PLANNING**

| | |
|---|---|
| Vancouver | Canada |
| Vienna | Austria |

CHAPTER 3.2
**WALKABLE COMMUNITIES**

| | |
|---|---|
| Pearl District, Portland | USA |
| Leipzig city centre and Plagwitz | Germany |

CHAPTER 3.3
**NEIGHBOURHOOD BUILDING BLOCKS**

| | |
|---|---|
| 'Mehr als Wohnen' and Kalkbreite, Zürich | Switzerland |
| Fruitvale, Oakland | USA |

CHAPTER 3.4
**MOVEMENT NETWORKS**

| | |
|---|---|
| Berliner Platz, Essen | Germany |
| Oklahoma City | USA |

CHAPTER 3.5
**ENVIRONMENTAL INTEGRATION**

| | |
|---|---|
| Singapore | Singapore |
| London | UK |

CHAPTER 3.6
**COMMUNITY EMPOWERMENT**

| | |
|---|---|
| Capitol Hill, Seattle | USA |
| Upper Calder Valley, Yorkshire | UK |

# CHAPTER 3.1
# URBAN PLANNING

**CASE STUDIES**
- Vancouver, Canada
- Vienna, Austria

- Active travel is limited when dispersed uses lead to car dependency.
- Compact mixed-use urban structures allow shorter travel distances and easier mobility.
- This leads to reduced congestion, better air quality and healthier lifestyles.

*'In short, I shall be writing about how cities work in real life, because this is the only way to learn what principles of planning and what practices in rebuilding can promote social and economic vitality in cities, and what practices and principles will deaden these attributes.'*

**JANE JACOBS**

*The Death and Life of Great American Cities*[1]

## INTRODUCTION

A series of principles for the organisation of large scale, strategic urban planning can help to create the conditions for us to lead healthier lives. The way settlements are laid out creates patterns that, once established, are hard to change and will influence the way people's lives are led far into the future. Looking at some typical patterns reveals how different the layouts of cities can be. They may be 'monocentric' as in Moscow and Vienna which have definite urban cores, 'polycentric' like London or Berlin, which are based on an aggregation of many villages, or they may be positioned in an 'isotropic grid', like New York City, where areas of local interest have become established within the regular background of the street formation.

**MONOCENTRIC**

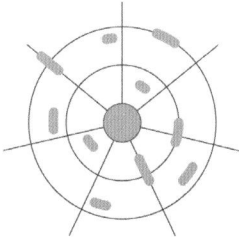

# MONOCENTRIC

- Such as Moscow, Vienna
- Plan based on radial and concentric movement pattern:
  - Increased pressure on city centre as single focus whose iconic heart emphasises power.
  - Many options for creation of local centres and walkable communities but challenging to break free from rigorous geometry.
  - Establishment of human scale competes with monocentric geometry.
  - Green spaces can be incorporated within the overall pattern, or break it.
- Grand geometrical imperative dominating life at a human scale.

**POLYCENTRIC**

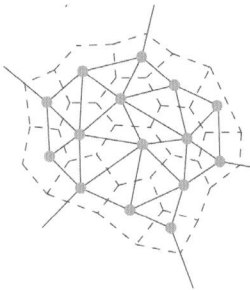

# POLYCENTRIC

- Such as London, Berlin
- A constellation of former villages responding to natural landscape features:
  - The overall layout evolves organically.
  - Walkable communities retain distinct historic names and identities.
  - Human scale is built into the neighbourhood concept.
  - Unplanned, circumstantially expedient movement pattern.
  - Green spaces including large areas of parkland influence.
- Excellent for neighbourhoods but with a serendipitous road system.

**GRID**

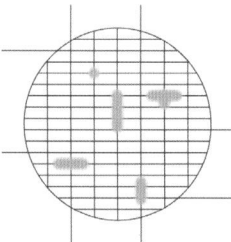

**FIGURE 3.1.1 A, B AND C**
Contrasting diagrams of city plan options: Monocentric, Polycentric and Isotropic Grid

# ISOTROPIC GRID

- Such as parts of many US cities
- A rigidly organised movement plan that is infinitely flexible:
  - In principle focal points can grow anywhere but are likely to be determined by constraints and/or opportunities in response to existing site features.
  - No clear boundaries within grid to define break-down into walkable communities.
  - Human scale has to assert itself as the grid is predicated on a logic of its own.
  - Green spaces can fit the grid or break it.
- Great flexibility yet limited by the regularity of right-angles.

**FIGURE 3.1.2 A, B AND C**
Figure-ground plans
of Amsterdam, Lisbon,
Barcelona

Figure 3.1.1 illustrates these contrasting patterns by simple depictions of road systems and centres of human activity. The dashed lines of the polycentric plan outline the neighbourhoods that are the hallmark of its system. But there are very few circumstances under which diagrams such as those illustrated would be adhered to, chapter and verse, as large settlements are likely to consist of several typologies. Over time, the changing circumstances in towns and cities have led to different arrangements, introducing variety and identity that might otherwise be lacking within the overall settlement.

Figure 3.1.2 is a selection of figure-ground plans of the cities of Amsterdam, Lisbon and Barcelona that illustrate the rich diversity that can develop over time.

Urban layouts are both constrained and enhanced by natural features which may relate to topography, geology, water courses, fields, forests and local microclimates. These can become defining factors for the identity of each place, onto which human customs such as religious worship, manufacture, commerce, culture, higher education and local traditions are overlaid.

Depending on how communities decide to use the urban spaces, these simple, conceptual diagrams have the potential to be made into very healthy or very unhealthy places to live in. For instance, whilst the grid may look mechanistic, and often is, shutting off routes in strategic locations can prevent traffic dominating the urban environment. The grid square plan suggests a relentless mass of development, but this can be avoided if some of the squares are developed as green spaces or the city has a river winding through it. The 'codebreaker' of New York City's Broadway is a further example.

The radial roads on the monocentric plan look rigid, but in Vienna each of them functions as the local high street for one of the eight districts outside the inner core. Having had very busy traffic in the past, sections of two of these arteries have been closed to private vehicles in the last five years and are now lively pedestrian spaces.

The polycentric plan may look disorganised, but the original villages could well have been founded to take advantage of natural features.

These examples demonstrate the diversity of city layouts that society has developed over time, which have been evolving ever more quickly in 21st-century cities, creating new challenges that need to be addressed. To do so, the patterns of urban environments will need to adapt if they are to accommodate our most important priorities. If individual and public health are prioritised as essential considerations, the way urban space is used in the future will need to adapt in response to the new understanding gained from rigorous research, analysis and sheer common sense.

## ACTIVE TRAVEL IS LIMITED WHEN DISPERSED USES LEAD TO CAR DEPENDENCY

Private vehicles contribute innumerable positive aspects to our lives, but it is equally important that we take note of the situations when they become a liability, and that we keep an open mind as to the best ways to overcome the challenges they present.

Figure 3.1.3, the diagram of dispersed and united uses, illustrates the problems faced when the primary destinations around which daily life revolves are far apart and time-consuming to reach. This is a characteristic of low-density settlements which generate insufficient ridership for public transport services both to be dependable for residents to use and viable for operators to provide. The dispersed arrangement is likely to lead to car dependency, causing journeys to be inefficient due to the difficulty of incorporating several

## DISPERSED AND UNITED USES

Low densities make public transport unviable and cause people to build their lives around their cars

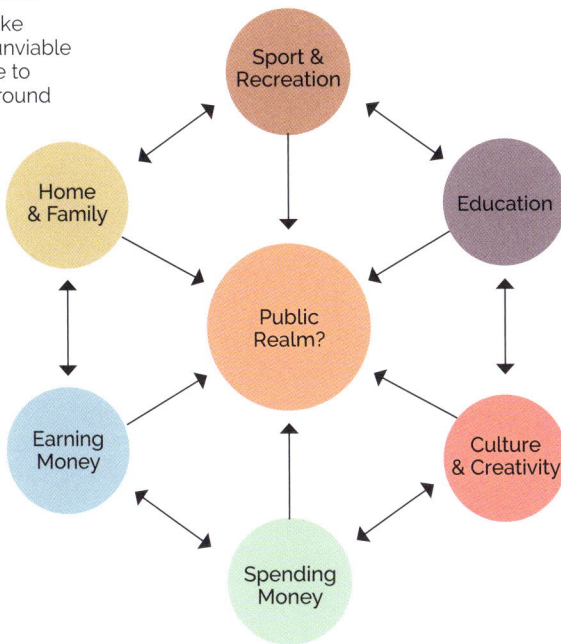

Sport & Recreation

Education

Home & Family

Public Realm?

Earning Money

Culture & Creativity

Spending Money

An intergrated mixed-use, public realm combines physical activity with commutity cohesion:
- healthier lifestyles
- reduced congestion
- better air quality
- interesting places
- great quality of life
- a healthy planet.

**FIGURE 3.1.3**
The problem with dispersed destinations and the advantages of united ones

destinations in one journey. A lack of vitality and social interaction means that any areas of public realm are less likely to be places in which to congregate, and the time spent driving reduces the opportunities for regular physical exercise to be a part of daily life.

As shown in the second diagram, the natural way to overcome these disadvantages is for the uses to be grouped together so that daily activities can be carried out using active travel on foot, by bicycle or public transport, making the process easier, more efficient and less time-consuming. The inclusion of 'home and family' amongst the uses is the single most important factor in enabling this to work effectively, due to the many health benefits already mentioned.

## THE PRIVATE CAR AND ACTIVE TRAVEL

Avoiding car dependency and creating a clear distinction between car ownership and car use is relevant to healthy placemaking, because of the huge number of vehicles on our roads and the lack of discrimination in how they are used. The environments created by the infrastructure built to serve those needs marginalise too many other important aspects of our lives.

A UN Habitat report from 2013, as relevant now as it was then, weighed up the pros and cons of the extent to which the private car dominates our lifestyles: 'The perceived advantages of convenience, privacy and status continue to make the private car an attractive means of urban transport... However a considerable range of externalities arise from increased motorization in cities, thus dwarfing its benefits. Being heavily dependent on oil, one of the most significant impacts of private motorised transport is on the environment, health and safety.'[2]

When full cars on long-distance journeys drive at maximum permitted speeds on uncongested roads they are in their element, and there is no reason why this should not continue to be the case for years to come. But, nearing a town or city, the spatial challenge is to work out where transitions in the urban structure can take place; the point where congested streets and problems finding parking spaces mean cars cease to be an asset and start to be a liability. The management and location of where people are permitted to park their cars is the key, as it is pointless to drive a vehicle to a destination where there is nowhere to leave it. For each existing settlement the location of that threshold will be specific to its unique layout. For a new settlement it can be designed from the outset.

Reducing parking space may raise objections about lost freedom of choice, disruption of established daily routines, warnings from retailers about loss of business and from economists about the decline of urban centres. Whilst some citizens may simply drive to nearby destinations where parking space is available, the choice to be made is between travelling elsewhere and the attractions of spending time in stimulating, well-designed places. Such environments have been introduced successfully in many cities and the key feature is to have easy and attractive ways to access them by sustainable, active travel. Mainland Europe has led the way in this respect, with places such as Copenhagen, Amsterdam, Vienna, Turin, Freiburg, Leipzig and Tübingen being good examples.

The private car belongs in a category of its own because driving, being so integral to their lives, can make people resistant to considering other ways of getting about. To be car-dependent means having either no alternative at all or believing that the alternatives on offer are too inconvenient and the infrastructure to support them too limited. As Jeff Tumlin pointed out in his book *Sustainable Transportation Planning*: 'The singular focus on moving cars has become so ingrained in our habits of thought that any mode other than an automobile may now be described as an "alternative" mode.'[3]

When people leave the car parked at home and choose to walk, cycle or use public transport, apart from the long-term health benefits they get from the exercise, they experience less traffic congestion, cleaner air, more and better opportunities for social interaction and fewer accidents. That is the basis for the concept of the 'Complete Street', summarised by Tumlin as: 'Designed for safe, comfortable and convenient movement both along and across the right-of-way by people of all ages and abilities, using multiple modes.'[4]

As regards the lack of feasible alternatives, planners need to recognise that the private car in motion is by far the most land-hungry form of transport and greatest cause of congestion, as well as neutralising large amounts of valuable urban space with car parking. It is obvious that buses and trams in the urban environment would be faster and more frequent if freed from congestion because the drivers had left their cars at home and were riding on board. This, and other movement related issues, are explored in more detail in Chapter 3.4.

## COMPACT MIXED-USE URBAN STRUCTURES ALLOW SHORTER TRAVEL DISTANCES AND EASIER MOBILITY

### RESTRUCTURING SETTLEMENTS
### TO MAKE URBAN CENTRES HEALTHIER

The way we use and value space in our settlements has been subject to change over time. Traditional settlements were laid out on a human scale, consisting of buildings accessed by streets and squares to facilitate circulation and congregation. The basic pattern is robust and has taken change 'in its stride' as settlements have grown into towns, cities and metropolises.

It is relevant to compare the basis on which vehicles are permitted to gain access to settlements with the way infrastructure services are provided. The management of utilities such as gas, water and electricity is by circulation between settlements at high pressure or voltage before being slowed to the levels required to serve domestic use. Aeroplanes and trains are managed on similar principles, with passengers changing transport modes on arrival to suit the human-scale environment.

When drivers leave the motorway and head into town, their expectations are to go right to the centre to find somewhere to park and, for many decades, the layouts of most settlements have been customised to fulfil this expectation. But this needs to be reformed by the introduction of thresholds in the layout of settlements where changes of transport mode are required to rebalance the movement system in urban centres. This would represent the vehicular version of adjusting to a human scale, and would lead to a more compact urban structure that can take advantage of the space liberated due to the reduction of that taken up by private vehicles, in motion and parked.

There is a wealth of documentation about traffic management, a subject that has fundamental impacts on the way our settlements have been developed. Starting in the mid-20th century the planning of cities, towns and villages has been car-centric whilst citizens' health has focused more on medical conditions than on lifestyles. In recent decades the balance between these two factors has begun to shift in recognition of the health risks caused by the lifestyle choices people make.

## EQUITABLE USE OF SPACE

Figure 3.1.4, the conceptual 'equitable use of space' diagram, shows that whilst the more expansive spaces in the outer zones of settlements involve longer travel distances suited to (non-polluting) vehicular traffic, there comes a tipping point beyond which it is counterproductive and antisocial for private vehicle traffic to go any further towards the centre. The converging arrows indicate some of the other categories of people who may wish to make use of the wide range of facilities on offer in the 'walkable core', and the appropriate modes of active travel for accessing them. The arrows also illustrate how space becomes increasingly valuable, and contested, the closer one gets to the urban core.

**FIGURE 3.1.4**
Equitable use of space

(A) **The open road**
Vehicles in their element

(B) **Settlement edge mixed-use neighbourhoods**
Space plentiful

(C) **Inner mixed-use neighbourhoods**
Space more contested

(D) **Transition gateways**
Transport mode changes, e.g. clean park and ride

(E) **Transition quarter mixed-use neighbourhoods**
Adjacent to core – residents' clean vehicles only

(F) **Walkable core mixed-use neighbourhoods**
Residents' clean vehicles only

→ Walk
→ Cycle
→ Public Transport
→ Drive

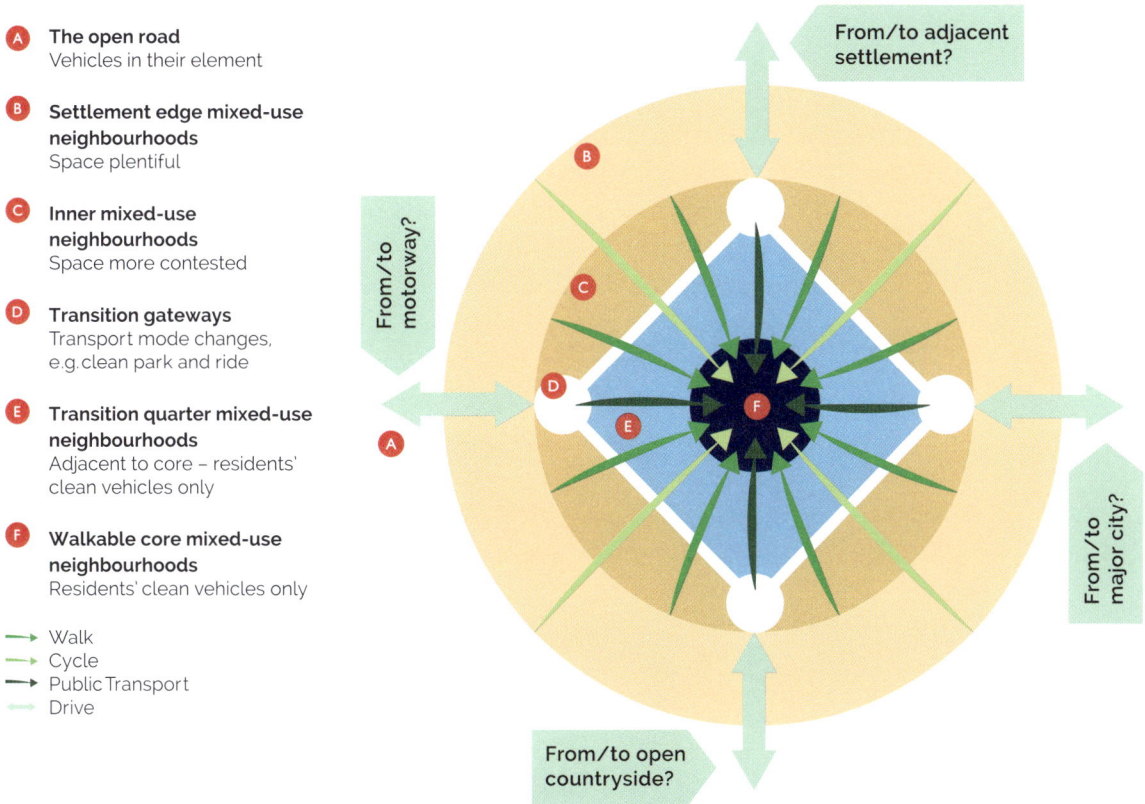

From/to adjacent settlement?

From/to motorway?

From/to major city?

From/to open countryside?

Expanding on the key to the diagram:

A. **The open road** is where vehicles are in their element, travelling at speed to a variety of possible destinations.

B. **Settlement edge mixed-use neighbourhoods** occupy peripheral areas of land where residential densities would be at the low end of the scale. Space would be plentiful enough for people to travel by car if necessary but, as the housing areas would all be walkable neighbourhoods, the amount of internal traffic would be less.

C. **Housing in the inner mixed-use neighbourhoods** would be at a higher density than in the settlement edge and space would be at more of a premium. But being sufficiently far from the settlement centre, traffic congestion would be limited and vehicle speeds reasonable.

D. **The transition gateways** are the thresholds beyond which private vehicles arriving from external locations are not permitted and whose further progress towards the settlement centre needs to be by less space-hungry travel modes. These can be by use of public transport (including taxis) bicycles or on foot. Park and Ride is the typical approach adopted by many towns and cities to serve this function.

E. The only private vehicles allowed to go beyond the **Transition gateways** are those of the residents living in the **Transition quarter mixed-use neighbourhoods**. Their proximity to the urban core implies higher densities and lower car ownership.

F. Residents of the **Walkable core mixed-use neighbourhoods** would also be permitted to bring their cars into the centre but, as is the case with many urban contexts, ownership may be low and vehicle use limited to the occasions when specific journeys are undertaken.

The location of Park and Ride facilities where land is less intensively used and of lower value, when supported by efficient shuttle bus systems, can be a simple solution that serves not only commuters but also those coming and going throughout the day.

This approach is of particular relevance regarding people living well away from the urban core in low-density neighbourhoods yet having the right to drive all the way into the centre where other citizens are leading their lives. As Brent Toderian points out: 'Though the status quo of big, bland, car-centric subdivisions retains enormous inertia, there is now a real counter-movement of urbanists trying to reclaim the virtues of pre-car towns and cities: scale, character, and walkability. As low-density developments become a drain on regional budgets — the infrastructure and service costs exceed the tax revenue — city officials are listening.'[5]

## REDUCED CONGESTION LEADS TO BETTER AIR QUALITY AND HEALTHIER LIFESTYLES

### ECONOMIC ASSESSMENTS

The adaptation of urban space as proposed in the 'equitable use of space' diagram, Figure 3.1.4, aims to restore the balance that has been progressively eroded by decades of vehicle-dominated city planning, and it is in the public realm that the majority of change would be experienced. The setting of public and private buildings will be enhanced by the creative re-purposing of the large amounts of space made available by reducing the quantum of motor vehicles. This should be easy to justify because of the urgent need to eradicate the poor air quality caused by vehicle congestion that leads to such a wide range of public health impacts.

Traffic congestion is a further cause for concern, a problem exacerbated by the large numbers of vehicles circulating in search of a parking place. UN Habitat reinforces the issue by pointing to its economic consequences: 'A further externality of private motorised transport is traffic congestion, which imposes significant costs on economic efficiency through reduced productivity.'[6] The economic impacts of congestion on individuals and businesses have been estimated by many organisations. The results vary depending on the methodologies used for calculation, but one carried out by Inrix, based on analysis estimating the total costs to the average driver in a city, arrives at a combination of direct and indirect costs of congestion to all UK motorists amounting to over £37.7 billion in 2017, an average of £1,168 per driver.[7]

Allowing too many vehicles to converge on urban centres is undesirable for the reasons set out above and needs to be addressed as a matter of urgency. Risks to health caused by poor air quality can cause respiratory illnesses and dementia, and the use of motor vehicles discourages active travel, meaning that less exercise is taken in daily life. It also limits the economic potential of cities due to the time lost due to traffic congestion. The conclusions of this analysis can be summarised by the following interrelated principles to guide decision-making on strategic planning projects:

Major public and employment centres should be located on public transport arteries and termini, to enable employees and visitors to access them using active travel rather than by car. Combined with the economic benefits of reduced congestion and less space occupied by vehicle parking, this will cut toxic emissions from vehicles and offer the health benefits of better air quality and exercise in daily life. This should be supported by creating corridors of sufficient residential density for public transport to be frequent and dependable and encourage active travel to reduce the car dependency that results from urban sprawl.

Easy access to high quality green spaces should be provided to enable everyone to benefit from the multiple health benefits already mentioned in Chapter 1. Settlement patterns must consist of mixed-uses laid out to make walking the natural choice for accessing the facilities that support daily life, and be designed to provide an attractive and stimulating public realm. These measures offer regular exercise, good air quality and social interaction.

This summary is an example of the connected strategies that are the bedrock of healthy placemaking by addressing a wide range of health risks through the introduction of planning concepts that are beneficial to the structure of settlements.

# KEY LESSONS

**SAVING COSTS OF HEALTH AND TECHNICAL INFRASTRUCTURE AND REDUCING CLIMATE CHANGE IMPACTS.**
Good governance by regional and city authorities must place healthy lifestyles as a top priority, avoiding the problems of urban sprawl, lengthy commuting and traffic congestion and improving citizens' wellbeing. The reduction in vehicle emissions will help to combat climate change.

**THE BENEFITS OF PHYSICAL EXERCISE IN DAILY LIFE, TO REDUCE LIFESTYLE RELATED, AVOIDABLE ILLNESSES.**
To be well-planned, settlements must be compact and consist of an integrated mix of uses including residential densities high enough to make ridership of clean public transport networks viable and reliable, and for active travel to be the natural choice for mobility.

**SOCIAL INTERACTION THAT BUILDS COMMUNITY AND SUPPORTS THOSE WITH MENTAL HEALTH DIFFICULTIES.**
Important destinations, including social, cultural, employment, leisure and retail facilities, must be conveniently located to create an efficient, functional and economically robust 'city of short distances' that reduces the trips made by car and encourages inclusive, vibrant neighbourhoods.

**HOW TO REALISE THESE QUALITIES BY DESIGN?**
- Impose controls on vehicles entering urban centres to overcome problems caused by traffic congestion and to make the environment healthier and more interesting.
- Establish the equitable use of urban space, including compulsory Park and Ride for vehicles arriving from destinations outside the settlement.
- Encourage the 'Complete Street' concept that regards all users as being of equal importance by rebalancing the space allocated to vehicles in favour of public transport, cyclists and pedestrians.

- Incorporate well-distributed local green spaces accessible to all residential areas within 10 minutes' walk, and strategic, settlement-wide green/blue areas serving the overall population.
- Create walkable, mixed-use neighbourhoods where there is a reduced need to drive to local shops and social facilities.
- Make arrangements that encourage active travel.
- Create attractive areas of public realm to encourage social interaction and build community.
- Ensure that all vehicles are free of fossil fuels and travel at low speeds in urban centres, for safety and to limit emissions of PM 2.5, the particulates caused by brakes, tyres and the road surface itself.
- Allow emergency vehicles as necessary and permit commercial vehicle access only at controlled times.

# CASE STUDY 3.1.1
# VANCOUVER, CANADA

## OVERVIEW: 'VANCOUVERISM'

In recent years Vancouver has been cited as one of the world's most liveable cities, a result of bold strategic planning decisions. Vancouver's population is 600,000 in the centre, rising to 2.3 million in the wider area. To prevent the urban sprawl that was creeping up the mountainsides overlooking the city, the planners introduced a densification programme for the city centre. This was based on tall apartment buildings whose residents could benefit from spectacular views of the still uncluttered mountains.

This was a clever and simple connected strategy that protected the natural environment and views onto it whilst generating a vibrant and successful downtown benefitting from excellent public transit serving large numbers of people. The high-rise blocks were configured to maintain views whilst avoiding undue inter-visibility or lack of privacy between apartments. This far-sighted

**FIGURE 3.1.6** A rich variety of thoughtfully-positioned buildings

**FIGURE 3.1.7** The lively streetscape with mixed-use frontage and residential towers above

**FIGURE 3.1.8**
Vancouver's Chinatown is a sociable and lively place

approach seems to have endowed the city with a sustainable, timeless quality and the overall impression is that Vancouver's response to the six healthy placemaking principles is very positive.

## VARIATIONS IN HEIGHT

Big cities are known for their tall, commercial towers and hotels but in Vancouver these are accompanied by large numbers of high-rise, residential blocks rising up to thirty and even fifty storeys. These are not confined to the downtown as they are distributed across otherwise low-rise, outlying districts such as Surrey, Burnaby, Richmond and New Westminster, increasing their density and helping them to become livelier places. What is different about the downtown, with its consistent, dense North American street grid, is the way its towers are set back from a base of low or medium-rise, mixed-use buildings. These line the busy streets and offer a human scale and greater variety of urban form, a characteristic maintained by areas of lower, more intimate residential accommodation.

## DIVERSE CHARACTER

Old buildings remain along major streets, reinforcing local identity, and former commercial loading bays create an appealing street cross-section for eateries and retail, with walkways raised a metre or so above street level forming promenades unencumbered by the cars parked below. Vancouver's cultural heritage is also reflected in the varied social environment, strongly

**FIGURE 3.1.9** Integration of greenery and residential towers with great views

represented by the Pacific east coast. These are mainly from China and Japan, and notable for the extensive choice of good grocery stores and places to eat catering for a range of income levels that serve as the bedrock for lower income communities. The social environment boasts a wide range of cultural and sporting facilities, and the rich variety of streetscapes has a further element in the form of narrow service roads behind the main street frontages that, whilst in themselves often unattractive, are very practical 'back-of-house' facilities which enable the primary public routes to be free of service yards.

## LIVEABILITY AND HEALTH

As a case study, Vancouver's qualities offer a solid basis of health benefits, particularly in the city centre. The city has an excellent public transit system fed by the high residential densities that serve vibrant, mixed uses along streets, creating a walkable, downtown environment where pedestrians and cyclists feel reasonably well respected and safe. These are complemented by an abundance of larger and smaller-scale green spaces, and by view corridors that maintain outlooks onto the wealth of waterbodies and across the water to the

**FIGURE 3.1.10** Yorktown's raised promenade creates an attractive setting

surrounding mountain ranges. The spacing of the residential towers is generous, offering privacy and avoiding overlooking. A benefit of the overall urban structure is that air quality seems reasonable partly due to the relative lack of street 'canyons', fairly low levels of vehicle traffic and assisted by the city's close proximity to waterbodies and green spaces. Headlines were created in August 2018 when air pollution in the city became dangerously high due to wildfires in the nearby forests, but to date this does not appear to have been a recurring problem.

The density of commercial activity offers stimulation and walkability which, in conjunction with the public transit services, means that car use is relatively low; Vancouver is the only North American city that has rejected urban freeways, although the Greater Vancouver region did not. Amongst the modern towers a large number of older buildings have been retained, a combination that adds up to an agreeable sense of place.

## AREAS FOR IMPROVEMENT

Major cities will always have their less desirable aspects and, as is the case with many of the most successful North American cities, Vancouver has downtown areas to which homeless people are drawn and 'the street becomes their living room'. The combination of the city's wealth and the relative mildness of the marine climate makes it attractive to the homeless, many of whom suffer from mental health problems. This creates a stark contrast that accentuates the inequalities that persist.

Despite the extensive public transit system that serves the vibrant, walkable downtown, cars are dominant in the lower density districts that surround it, leading to wide roads and extensive parking lots for out of town retail centres.

# CASE STUDY 3.1.2
# VIENNA, AUSTRIA

**FIGURE 3.1.11**
The multimodal Ringstrasse
encircles Vienna's 1st District

## OVERVIEW

Like Vancouver, Vienna (population 1.9 million) is counted amongst the world's most liveable cities and has a clarity of layout that enables it to function extremely well without feeling in any way regimented. A centre for culture, learning, art, music, architecture – and the birthplace of psychoanalysis – Vienna is one of Europe's most iconic cities.

An ancient city whose tumultuous history includes fending off Ottoman invasions in the 16th century, Vienna's heyday was as the capital of the Austro-Hungarian Empire and centre of Art Nouveau extravagance during the Secession at the turn of the 19th century. Four huge, concrete 'Flak' towers still remain in city parks as reminders of dark times in WW2. Since the end of the Cold War in the closing decades of the 20th century, the city has seen major regeneration and expansion, looking east towards Bratislava and Budapest.

**FIGURE 3.1.12** The elegant, bustling Graben

**FIGURE 3.1.13** The pedestrianised section of Mariahilfer Strasse

**FIGURE 3.1.14** Lakeside Aspern Seestadt combines imaginative apartments with strong environmental credentials

## THE RINGSTRASSE AND 1ST DISTRICT

The Ringstrasse defines the central 1st District with the cathedral of Stephansdom at its heart, its spire representing the city's 'axis mundi'. Built in the 1850s, the Ringstrasse transformed the city's, by then redundant, fortifications into a spacious tree-lined boulevard that connects rather than separates. It is punctuated by a series of civic buildings created during the period of the Austro-Hungarian Empire, including the State Opera, the Parliament, the State Theatre, the University, the Natural History and Art Museums and the Town Hall. The 1st District has a walkable diameter of 1.5 km. Tram services along the Ringstrasse offer pedestrian access into the city centre from whichever side is most convenient, allowing the central area to have limited vehicular traffic and the historic core to retain much of its original character.

## URBAN STRUCTURE

The city has a very legible, concentric urban structure consisting of a network of radial routes intersected by ring roads. The radial routes are a series of thoroughfares leading out from the Ringstrasse, serving as 'high streets' for eight inner districts that are bounded by the Gürtel (belt) beyond which twelve outer districts encircle the city. The extensive public transport network follows the street geometries, interwoven with the Stadtbahn with its iconic station buildings designed by Otto Wagner. The U-Bahn (underground) system was begun in the 1970s and the city has introduced policies to

**FIGURE 3.1.15**
Looking towards the
Wienerwald from the Donau
Kanal

reduce car use and prioritise cycling. This includes blocking parts of at least
two of the major radial routes to traffic (Mariahilfer Strasse and Landstrasser
Hauptstrasse) to create fully pedestrianised zones whose vitality has
naturally blossomed. Lively public markets such as the Naschmarkt and
Rochusmarkt are important places for social interaction in attractive,
distinctive settings.

## GREEN/BLUE INFRASTRUCTURE

The Donau Kanal (Danube Canal) defines the eastern edge of the 1st District
with waterside foot and cycle routes, and facilities for outdoor swimming,
volley-ball etc. Further east is the Danube itself, supplying further magnets
for recreation along its banks. The Wienerwald (Vienna Woods) rising up to
the west and north of the city provides extensive areas for walks with views
back over the generally low- and mid-rise city.

**FIGURE 3.1.16** Part of Vienna's new University of Economics and Business

## GOVERNANCE

The city's governance is effective and has set realistic targets for accommodating population growth based on ecologically-guided principles and providing social infrastructure facilities. 50% of the land within the city boundary is green space and this ratio will be retained despite the city's population growth requiring an additional 130,000 dwellings by 2025. It is to be achieved by renovating older housing, densifying existing areas and creating new neighbourhoods. Air quality is generally good and the city is well-provided with public parks at varying scales as well as set-piece historic palaces such as the Belvedere and Schönbrunn. It has also been upgrading its railway infrastructure to act as the catalyst for mixed-use, transport-orientated developments, and has been built an unashamedly modern new University of Economics and Business.

## AREAS FOR IMPROVEMENT

Vienna still has high levels of vehicular traffic on multi-lane highways such as the Gürtel outer ring road and some parts of the Ringstrasse itself, resulting in places where pedestrians can feel somewhat marooned. And despite the city's concerted efforts to see an increase in the number of cycle trips this has not been as successful as hoped.

CHAPTER 3.2
# WALKABLE COMMUNITIES

**CASE STUDIES**

- Pearl District, Portland, USA
- Leipzig city centre and Plagwitz, Germany

- Motor vehicles, whether in motion or parked, take up too much space in our settlements.
- We walk or cycle when our daily needs are easy to reach, benefitting from the exercise and saving time.
- A lively and attractive public realm is stimulating and promotes social interaction.

*'The truth is that it has to do with the quality of the design. People will walk longer if it's a pleasant environment and they won't walk at all if it's harsh or unsafe.'*

**BRENT TODERIAN**[1]

## INTRODUCTION

The larger scale strategies set out in the previous chapter on urban planning pave the way to the benefits of walkable communities, as walkability is the keystone of healthy placemaking.

There are many advantages in living somewhere that enables us to walk to all the places we need to access as part of daily life; local shops, health facilities, schools, workplaces, places to meet, eat and drink, green spaces for play, for relaxation and for growing food. A well-designed walkable community or neighbourhood is the fundamental concept at the heart of healthy placemaking. It must function as an integrated system whose component parts create a healthy environment that enhances the wellbeing of its inhabitants. Its pattern was established when *Homo sapiens* first started to live communally, as is evident in countless existing settlements, and it continues to be valid and relevant today.

Citizens may be categorised as commuters, cyclists or pedestrians but can be any or all of these at different times of day, year and stages of life. Awareness of this helps us break down rigid definitions of users of the public realm and ensures that urban space is organised to strike an equitable balance serving the needs of all stakeholders. When daily needs can be reached on foot the need for car access and parking is lower, making the place compact and therefore all the more walkable. This helps to build trust and create a sense of community, enabling frequent, chance meetings where matters of local interest can be aired that make the place resilient and healthy – mentally as well as physically.

## MOTOR VEHICLES, WHETHER IN MOTION OR PARKED, TAKE UP TOO MUCH SPACE IN OUR SETTLEMENTS

Cars are mobile pieces of people's private space which they are entitled to use in the public realm. The need for parking provision in settlements is upheld by planning systems that require transport authorities to deliver space for cars when in motion and more space for them when parked whilst drivers go about their business. Urban spaces originally used for congregation have often been re-purposed as car parks, based on the assumption that this was a pre-requisite for a thriving, future-orientated economy.

But urban land occupied by vehicle infrastructure fragments the layout of the destinations the drivers have come to visit, making it less convenient and the environment less attractive. Settlement structures have centres and when too many vehicles try to access and park in them at the same time the quality of the urban environment plummets as a platform for human activity.

When less space is occupied by parking the urban structure can be more compact, distances shorter and the need to use vehicles reduced. The healthiest urban centres have a mix of uses that includes residential accommodation, for whose occupants the main use of their cars, if they have them, is to travel out of town. These citizens have the right to breathe clean air, and the spaces currently occupied by car parking in public urban areas have potential to be used in other ways.

Figures 3.2.1 A and 3.2.1 .B illustrate work carried out by JTP for the Tulli area in Tampere, Finland's second city, where there is a lack of green space and many streets lack active frontages. Removal of the multi-storey car park, by relocating the parking below ground, frees-up the public realm for a new, green space that also opens up views to other areas. The cylindrical shape in the background of Figure 3.2.1.b is the car park's spiral ramp which is to be re-purposed as a play area or an art gallery.

## WE WALK OR CYCLE WHEN OUR DAILY NEEDS ARE EASY TO REACH, BENEFITTING FROM THE EXERCISE AND SAVING TIME

The focus of a walkable community is intentionally local, its goal being to create a cohesive social environment with a strong sense of identity. It recognises that many of its inhabitants may travel elsewhere to work, but others may work within the neighbourhood, in small businesses or from home. The key is to create a place within which people can carry out a substantial proportion of their day to day activities on foot and can do so in a way that makes the experience easy, safe and enjoyable.

In its document 'The Pedestrian Pound', Living Streets, the UK charity for everyday walking, makes the case for the many social and economic advantages of walkable environments, and also cites the employment benefits that accrue from a high quality public realm: 'public realm investment has been associated with increases in employment. In Dublin, the redevelopment of the Temple Bar District led to a 300% increase in employment before the economic boom.'[2]

Whether for the re-planning of an existing settlement or the creation of a new one, specialist retail and public services required less frequently must be positioned where they can serve several walkable communities or be located within larger-scale centres further afield. These may include hospitals, secondary schools or sports facilities. As this would cause the walkable community to become a destination attracting visitors from elsewhere it is important for the facility to be located away from the central core and close to

**FIGURE 3.2.1 A**
The existing street with a multi-storey car park

**FIGURE 3.2.1 B**
Bringing the space to life by replacing the car park with green space and turning the route into one for pedestrians and cyclists only

the main entry points. This is to avoid the unwanted impacts of concentrations of traffic and parking that would fragment the space and downgrade the environment. If important uses are already located in an urban centre, access to them must be using active travel, to avoid unnecessary traffic and space being wasted with areas of car parking.

## CREATING THE CONDITIONS
## FOR PEOPLE TO LEAD HEALTHY LIVES

Figure 3.2.2 illustrates a sequence that describes the basic ingredients on which walkable communities depend, the urban planning opportunities they offer, the successive effects they lead to and the health benefits they deliver. The descriptions relate these benefits to the conditions in typical urban contexts as currently experienced. The fundamental components that make up a walkable community are inter-dependent; all of them must be present to support one another and deliver the sequence of health benefits they can generate:

1. a compact, mixed-use urban structure
2. daily needs (i.e. shops, healthcare, primary school) within walking distance
3. integrated green space.

## WALKABLE COMMUNITIES

A compact mixed-use urban structure in a central location that incorporates shops, services, social facilities, a range of employment spaces and a substantial quantum of mixed-tenure, residential accommodation provides the basic elements required for a community to function.

The mixed-use centre is in itself dependent on these daily needs being within comfortable walking distance of the areas of housing, as it removes the need for them to be accessed by private motor vehicles. This is the key to the compactness that makes for a lively public realm.

The integration of green space makes a vital contribution to the quality of life within the community. It enhances the public realm with greenery on streets and in public spaces, planting associated with amenity space for apartments and places for recreation and also allotments, orchards and private gardens.

These three elements form the basis for the following outcomes that promote health and wellbeing:

**PATHS TO THE FUTURE – LESS VEHICLE TRAFFIC, ACTIVE TRAVEL ENCOURAGED, ENHANCED SOCIAL INTERACTION, IMPROVED PUBLIC REALM**

The impact of private vehicles is minimised in the compact, walkable, traffic-calmed centre and the emphasis on movement patterns will be on the many options for active travel. This improves the quality of the public realm and leads to lively social environments.

**POSITIVE OUTCOMES – FEWER TRAFFIC ACCIDENTS, BREATHE FRESHER AIR, EXERCISE OUTDOORS, RESILIENT COMMUNITIES, EXPERIENCING NATURE**

With fewer private vehicles, and travelling at low speeds, the likelihood of traffic accidents is reduced. Less traffic means better air quality which is enhanced by the integrated green spaces that will also be beneficial for experiencing nature and taking physical exercise outdoors, all helping to strengthen the sense of community.

**HEALTH BENEFITS – HEALTHIER LIMBS, HEALTHIER LUNGS, HEALTHIER HEARTS, HEALTHIER MINDS**

Limbs will benefit from exercise in daily life as well as that taken in green spaces which will also benefit lungs due to the outdoor exercise and the clean air. Exercise and time spent in green space is good for the heart in reducing the risks of cardiovascular illnesses, type 2 diabetes and several forms of cancer. Social interaction in a lively public realm can help to maintain mental and physical health, as can spending time in green space and working alone, or with companions, in allotments.

With these elements in place, a sense of wellbeing can be gained from convenient and efficient access to the things around which people build their lives. The proximity of the amenities to where people live means that, without planning to, they get daily doses of physical exercise, social interaction and fresh air. In order to create a successful walkable community, designers and stakeholders must look to include the following elements:

## THE MOVEMENT FRAMEWORK

The area of an individual walkable community is limited by the distances people are willing to walk. On average, a 10-minute walk covers 750-800 m. This determines the radius of a walkable community. As shown in Figure 3.0.3 a series of walkable communities can be joined together to constitute a larger settlement. This basic pattern is flexible and can serve a wider movement network through public transport and other active travel modes such as cycling, which in 10 minutes covers 2 km and typically continues for much longer. In this way, the distance that can be travelled without depending on motor vehicles is extended.

The movement system must be safe and easy to navigate; a clear system of wayfinding based on landmarks and streets with distinctive character and with maximum vehicles speeds, in all urban areas, of 20 mph. Walking and cycling must be given the highest priority along with public transport, followed by business traffic and finally private vehicles. Space allocated to vehicular movement and parking should be minimised with the area gained being replaced by active travel modes; clean public transport, cycling that occupies little space in motion and parked, and walking which takes up the least amount of space. Delivery times for commercial vehicles must be controlled to keep clear of morning and evening traffic peaks as well as avoiding disruption to residents' sleep caused by engine noise and warning signals when reversing. Public

**HEALTH BENEFITS**
- Healthier limbs
- Healthier lungs
- Healthier hearts
- Healthier wellbeing

**POSITIVE OUTCOMES**
- Fewer traffic accidents
- Breathe fresher air
- Exercise outdoors
- Resilient communities
- Experiencing nature

**PATHS TO THE FUTURE**
- Less vehicle traffic
- 'Active travel' encouraged
- Enhanced social interaction
- Improved public realm

**WALKABLE COMMUNITIES**
- Integrated green space
- Daily needs within walking distance
- Compact, mixed-use urban structure

**FIGURE 3.2.2** Walkable Communities diagram

transport services must be sufficiently frequent for people to rely upon them. A maximum of 10-minute intervals means users can wait for the next to arrive with no need to consult timetables.

## FACILITIES AND SERVICES

The facilities within walking distance to serve daily needs during the day and in the evening must include a variety of shops and choices for food and beverages and leisure and entertainment facilities. Local businesses will have employees from the neighbourhood or elsewhere, who will make use of shops and eateries during the working day. Social facilities are needed for public or private meetings and may be combined with spaces for childcare and healthcare.

Primary schools must be close to the settlement centre, accessed on foot in safety and breathing clean air; the reason why drop-off areas should be avoided due to the associated health risks they cause. Secondary schools must be located where they can serve several walkable communities, and are best accessed by buses or on safe, segregated cycle routes with prioritised crossing points.

## A LIVING ENVIRONMENT

Homes need to reflect local housing need and are likely to require a range of residential typologies with a balanced mix of tenures and densities to serve people of all ages and walks of life. The public realm must be attractive, stimulating and accessible, with spaces designed with greenery, seating, children's play facilities, public artworks and places for events and celebrations. Green/blue spaces must provide areas for exercise, relaxation, fresh air, comfortable microclimates and rich biodiversity and should be linked by vehicle-free routes to other neighbourhoods.

# A LIVELY AND ATTRACTIVE PUBLIC REALM
# IS STIMULATING AND PROMOTES SOCIAL INTERACTION

**FIGURE 3.2.3 A**
The existing urban space

**FIGURE 3.2.3 B**
How the space could be
brought to life

A well-designed public realm with a strong identity attracts people when it offers a wide range of experiences to suit the tastes of all ages and cultures. When attention is captured by things people find interesting their wish to explore means they get the health benefits of physical exercise 'for free', even though they may have been neither planning to, nor conscious of doing so.

Strong identity can be a decisive factor in people's choices of where to spend time, and contact with the flavours of different cultures is one of the

**FIGURE 3.2.4**
Vieux Port Pavilion, Marseille

most compelling. In their various guises, such as New York's Little Italy and Chinatown and London's Brick Lane reflect the positive impacts of immigrant populations in any number of cities, whilst indigenous souks, bazaars and other forms of street market transform the process of buying things into an interesting experience. It does so by placing the intangible benefits of social interaction on an equal footing with the business of financial transactions.

The quality of the public realm in terms of layout, materials and elements such as public art, water features and play spaces is critical, as it must reach out to all sectors of the community if it is to be successful and self-sustaining. That quality depends on every part having something positive to offer, which is why the compactness of the urban structure is so important. The right balance of these factors creates levels of social interaction that build community and generate a sense of wellbeing.

Figures 3.2.3 A and 3.2.3 B illustrate how public realm improvements in the Tulli area of Tampere could transform an existing, underused space into a lively destination. The new public building at the back strengthens spatial enclosure and decoration makes the mundane façade of the building on the right more interesting. In the foreground, new lighting columns march along the main route and the street trees and planting beds improve the scale of the space and soften the large expanse of paving.

The installation of public art is an effective way to create a distinct identity and sense of culture in a community. The artworks can be identified as placemarkers to help orientation within the settlement and people can engage with them in direct and indirect ways, provoking discussion and reflection. In large cities they can prove popular tourist attractions, such as the Vieux Port Pavilion in Marseille designed by Foster + Partners, Figure 3.2.4, whilst in smaller towns they can become an important part of the social history, an example being the Henry Moore statues in Harlow, England.

## SHOPPING AND OTHER USES

The layout of many urban environments has been based on the assumption that city centres are primarily places for shopping and that shops depend on customer parking to be economically successful. But this has been questioned by research such as the material provided by 'The Means: to change places for the better' which states that 'Car drivers spend more on a single trip; walkers and bus users spend more over a week or a month. In 2011, in London town centres, walkers spent £147 more per month than those travelling by car. Compared with 2004, spending by public transport users and walkers has risen; spending by car users and cyclists has decreased'.[3] This can provide food for thought for all design professionals interested in creating places that combine economic success with good quality, and healthy, placemaking.

Much is made of the decline of town centres resulting from the growth of internet shopping. Whilst the internet clearly has an impact, there is a tendency for commentators to treat retail as the primary function of town centres and to bemoan their decline. This assumption can be overcome by regarding shopping not as an end in itself, but as one of a range of equally worthwhile activities and experiences where people can eat and drink, meet and greet, and enjoy events and entertainment as well as some 'retail therapy'. These experiences can be enhanced further by greenery and street furniture such as pavilions and pergolas.

**FIGURE 3.2.5**
Helsinki Esplanade
in summer

**FIGURE 3.2.6**
Helsinki Esplanade
in winter

Interventions can be made at any scale. Around City Hall in London are generous amounts of seating and greenery in a fully-pedestrianised space that attracts large numbers of people into the area. An example at a more modest scale is the pop-up seating created by Arup for FitzPark on Windmill Street in London's West End. These act as invitations to socialise and relax, and the ideas can inspire creativity amongst designers.

Living Streets' document 'Pedestrian Pound' continues on this theme, focusing on the contribution made by pedestrians to local economies when encouraged by public realm improvements: 'in Piccadilly, Stoke-on-Trent, a £10 million investment to make the area more pedestrian-friendly has increased footfall by 30%. Measures such as widening footpaths, replacing existing footpath surfaces, installing trees and seating has encouraged large numbers of people back to the town centre. New businesses, cafés and restaurants have opened. The project's success has led to further strategic investment in public realm improvements to boost business performance.'[4]

## ADAPTING TO THE WEATHER

Different climates around the world pose a variety of challenges but contact with the vagaries of weather is an essential aspect of people's lives. How healthy the places are depends on an understanding of how to respond to

**FIGURE 3.2.7**
Turin Colonnade

local circumstances, as settlements have been created in the most diverse, and ostensibly harsh, climatic conditions because people have prioritised their interest in living there over moving to somewhere that has a more comfortable climate.

These places– wet, dry, hot, cold or in-between– can all offer health benefits. Depending on local weather patterns, people make their environments comfortable by the installation of protection from sun, rain and snow with colonnades, and deal with hot and cold temperatures through the orientation of buildings, the width of streets and the planting of trees. The way wind is managed depends on whether the intention is to speed it up to keep buildings and spaces cool, or block it to keep them warm.

Urban design strategies of this kind offer a wealth of choices to adapt the weather to create comfortable micro-climates. Helsinki, despite its long, cold, dark winters has the centrally-located Esplanade, Figures 3.2.5 and 3.2.6, a stately public space whose use is maximised in the summer. During the winter people are more likely to congregate indoors in the Esplanade's cafés and restaurants, but the public space comes alive again in December with its vibrant Christmas Market. The Esplanade encourages walking and socialising with all its attendant health benefits.

The Italian city of Turin gets very hot in summer but the protection provided by its magnificent colonnades, Figure 3.2.7, makes it an ideal setting for the 'Passeggiata', the daily ritual where citizens parade in smart clothes, maintain social contacts and enjoy indulging in countless bars, cafés and restaurants or eating ice-cream. Whilst the diet may not be particularly healthy, the urban planning of the colonnades is a very clever, multifaceted system for health and wellbeing, that offers protection against the summer heat and winter's rain and snow, the daily exercise of walking and the social interaction generated by the overall environment.

An essential aspect of such places is their distinctiveness, whose unique qualities can generate a sense of belonging amongst the community and fascination for visitors, something that the designer can exploit by finding creative ways to combine urban planning and architecture with local culture.

# KEY LESSONS

### THE HEALTH BENEFITS OF WALKABLE COMMUNITIES

The combination of integrated green space, daily needs within walking distance and a compact, mixed-use urban structure provide the foundations for healthy neighbourhoods. Reduced need to use vehicles makes the public realm safer and more interesting, encouraging social interaction and making it easy to get exercise in daily life. Access to public green space is beneficial for physical and mental health and moderates the impacts of rain, wind and overheating.

### HIGH QUALITY PUBLIC REALM

People like to visit places that are interesting, stimulating and catch the imagination with a mix of retail outlets, events and many other attractions.

### AVOIDING ROAD ACCIDENTS AND RESPIRATORY ILLNESSES

Limited parking space and low vehicle speeds lead to safer streets and cause fewer injuries, traumas and fatalities. Air quality is improved when fossil fuel vehicles are banned in built-up areas.

### TAKE ACCOUNT OF THE CLIMATE AND LOCAL CULTURE

Climate and local culture are part of a place's identity which are attractive for visitors and can be exploited in design decisions.

## HOW TO REALISE THESE QUALITIES BY DESIGN?

- Create neighbourhood centres with a wide choice of mixed uses including shops, places to eat and drink, business premises, childcare and primary school facilities and spaces for meetings.
- Only permit housing development within 10-minutes' walk of neighbourhood centres or within 5-8 minutes' walk of public transport stops. The stops must offer a service to those centres that is sufficiently regular throughout the day for people to use it.
- Housing areas must be at a density that supports the viability of regular public transport, which in turn will disincentivise car ownership and minimise space allocated to parking.
- Make areas of public realm compact, as high quality construction materials are more affordable when the amount of space needed to be covered is smaller.
- Use imagination in designing environments that respond to the settlement's climate and reflect its local culture.
- Plant street trees to soften urban environments, absorb pollutants, attenuate rainwater runoff and limit the effects of urban heat islands.
- Create areas of high quality public realm by narrowing streets and widening pavements and reducing the space allocated to car parking.
- Encourage cycling into urban centres from longer distances by providing dedicated bicycle lanes.
- Ensure that the design of a walkable community lives up to its name.

# PEARL DISTRICT, PORTLAND, USA

**FIGURE 3.2.8**
Pearl District, aerial view showing mix of heights, uses and typologies

The site was a disused railway yard to the north of the downtown. A Rural Urban Design Assistance Team (RUDAT) Charrette in the early 1990s led to a neighbourhood association of local businesses that encouraged local ownership. Determined to realise their vision, the group lobbied successfully to change the area's zoning code from commercial to mixed-use. This enabled the collaborative local involvement of smart, committed people with their own visions which led to an overall pattern that worked for all stakeholders.

## A MIXED-USE NEIGHBOURHOOD

The Pearl District has an attractive, relaxed atmosphere composed of a mix of housing, employment leisure and entertainment. The district itself has an area of 150 acres (62 hectares) excluding the part that extends to the centre-line of the broad Willamette River. It is large enough to work as a neighbourhood,

**FIGURE 3.2.9** Pearl District, warehouse buildings converted into rowhouses

**FIGURE 3.2.10** Pearl District, Paseo instead of street

**FIGURE 3.2.11** Pearl District, streetcars imported from Sweden to negotiate fine-grain urban structure

pleasantly contained by the river frontage, and consists of a mix of historic and repurposed commercial buildings and new development that blend variety of scale and character. Building heights start low in the south and rise towards the river in the north, an overall pattern that relates to the city's structure and offers good solar orientation.

The mixed-use neighbourhood evolved naturally, beginning with small apartments targeted at pioneer, young couples who were expected to move elsewhere when starting families. When they wanted to stay on to enjoy life in the Pearl District, the experienced local developers showed flexibility by introducing areas of family housing that led to greater social diversity and a stronger sense of community.

## STREETS AND SPACES

Portland generally has 24 m (80 ft) wide north-south streets for good sunlight penetration where main entrances to buildings are located, and secondary entrances and parking garage accesses on 18 m (60 ft) wide, more shaded, east-west streets. Thoughtful use of the street grid allows for pedestrianised, green 'paseos' that alternate with vehicular routes.

The Pearl District has a more intimate, finer grain road system than the rest of the city, for which smaller streetcars, custom-made in Sweden, were imported. This suits the diversity of mixed uses along streets that incorporates low- and high-rise housing. Horticultural experts

**FIGURE 3.2.12** Pearl District, boardwalk sidewalk and sociability

**FIGURE 3.2.13** Pearl District, Tanner Springs Park taking cues from the site's history and Oregon's natural environments

planted street trees in continuous trenches to allow roots to spread more evenly, allowing for healthier trees and fewer problems of roots buckling sidewalk paving.

The neighbourhood has a variety of public spaces, some hard-landscaped and others mainly soft. This includes Tanner Springs Park, a green space designed by Studio Dreiseitl, that incorporates plants and shrubs native to the different climate zones within Oregon State. Along its eastern side is a functional and sustainable 'harmonious fence' using pieces of recycled railway track that embed the site's history into the new neighbourhood. Nearby is a stretch of sidewalk that is surfaced as a timber boardwalk whose contrast with the standard paving introduces variety as it leads north to the Fields Park green space.

# CASE STUDY 3.2.2
# CENTRAL LEIPZIG
# AND PLAGWITZ, GERMANY

## 1. CENTRAL LEIPZIG

Leipzig's population declined from 750,000 in 1939 to 590,000 at the time of Germany's partition, due to lack of employment, but its regeneration since the country's reunification has raised the number up to 770,000. During WW2 Leipzig suffered relatively little bomb damage, compared to other cities such as Dresden, and has gone to great lengths to restore and repurpose its many high quality buildings.

The city's successful recovery from former GDR times has led to a thriving economy given a new lease of life due to the return of citizens who had moved elsewhere after WW2 to find work. Leipzig's urban planning department developed a very coherent, future-orientated and, above all, deliverable

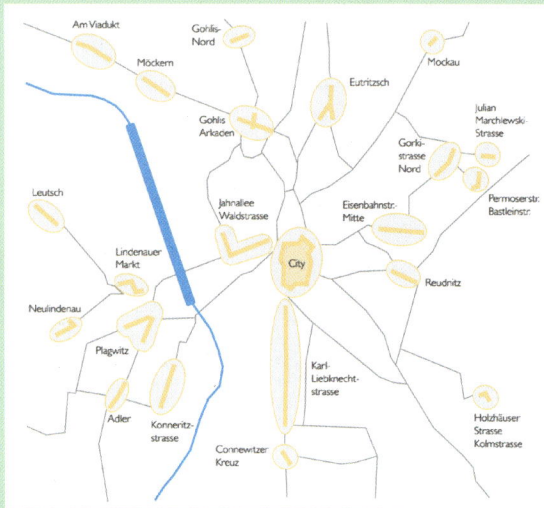

**FIGURE 3.2.15** Leipzig's city plan showing local centres based on walkable communities

**FIGURE 3.2.16** Leipzig's city plan showing local centres overlay (aerial photography © Google Earth)

strategy to regenerate the city. This was one of the many reasons it won the Academy of Urbanism's (AoU) 2019 European City of the Year Award.

## A WALKABLE CENTRE

Leipzig's centre works as a walkable heart, the 'Living Room' for the whole city that serves the local population and increasing numbers of tourists. The strategy for the surrounding neighbourhoods shows a series of local shopping streets spaced out at distances of 1-2 km, that can function as the centres of walkable communities.

The city centre measures approximately 900 m from north to south and 700 m from east to west, and retains many splendid, historic buildings, lovingly restored. In 2008 the area of car-free space in Leipzig's Living Room was increased by 40% to create a beautiful, compact and virtually car-free city centre with a series of linked, pedestrianised streets and squares. The variety of walkable and legible urban spaces includes fascinating passages through the urban blocks that date from the city's past as a destination for trade fairs.

**FIGURE 3.2.17** Leipzig Centre, Thomaswiese – a good place to relax

**FIGURE 3.2.18** Leipzig Centre, Naschmarkt – a convivial civic space

## TRANSPORT AND ENVIRONMENT

The magnificent mainline station is an interchange that connects with newly-created rail tunnels running under the city centre. These improve active mobility whilst preserving the iconic urban structure above and are integrated with the excellent, multi-modal public transport system connecting to outer suburbs.

The city's environmental measures consist of strategic broad green/blue swathes and an integrated network of footpaths and cycle routes, often following water bodies. To the south of the centre, a series of former lignite coal mines that created air and ground pollution have been cleaned up and transformed into lakes for recreation and biodiversity.

## AREAS FOR IMPROVEMENT

The ring road around the city centre creates a significant barrier to pedestrians and cyclists. There is talk of reducing the number of vehicle lanes to share the road spaces more equitably. As the European hub for DHL cargo flights, the city's airfield is permitted to function 24 hours a day. The overnight flights reduce the quality of life of small settlements nearby, but the city has no power to resolve this as it is a matter dealt with at federal level.

**FIGURE 3.2.19** Plagwitz, a safe green route to the city centre along a re-opened canal

**FIGURE 3.2.20**
Plagwitz, Josephstrasse is traffic-calmed and has a village-like feel

# 2. PLAGWITZ

At a neighbourhood level Leipzig has responded to the challenges of economic decline and depopulation in a way that empowers citizens and makes the most of scant resources. Groups of citizens have been encouraged to take over vacant buildings and act as 'guardians' with contracts for five or ten years. Walking around the neighbourhood of Plagwitz this approach looks very successful as the remaining, derelict buildings are brought back into service. Rents are rising, and land formerly used for gardens and social infrastructure is being reclaimed for development by owners.

## A GROWING COMMUNITY

Plagwitz is a former industrial area that is being transformed into a new, healthy, walkable community. The active regeneration of abandoned or war-damaged buildings, filling 'missing teeth', includes a variety of housing typologies in a mix of old and new buildings that create pleasant, human-scale streets suited to a diverse demographic mix. The built form is compact but with generous, tree-lined avenues for the trams that are the linchpin of Leipzig's 'active travel' strategy. The city is working with landowners to provide new social infrastructure such as kindergartens and schools, making great efforts to keep pace with the population growth resulting from the city's newfound attractiveness.

Karl-Heine-Strasse is a main artery with a lively mix of uses including retail, employment, places to eat and drink, social and cultural facilities and

**FIGURE 3.2.21**
Plagwitz, Karl-Heine-
Strasse – a tree-lined high
street with a tram service

residential accommodation on the upper floors. Its tram service forms part of an integrated public transport system that includes buses and provides excellent connections to the city centre and other neighbourhoods.

There are large areas of green space around the periphery of Plagwitz and several small ones in the interior, apparently decreasing in number. An attractive tree-lined green route along a refurbished canal offers car-free access to and from the city centre that is used for leisure as well as commuting.

## AREAS FOR IMPROVEMENT

• Despite Leipzig's admirable public transport infrastructure, the 1990s explosion of car use in the former GDR resulting from Germany's unification means neighbourhoods such as Plagwitz still have a lot of cars in motion and parked.
• Some narrow, pleasantly-proportioned, historic streets are now so lined with parked cars that it can be hard for vehicles to pass one another, especially when refuse lorries make their rounds.
• More green spaces in the interior of Plagwitz would improve quality of life and help to moderate the extremes of weather

# CHAPTER 3.3
# NEIGHBOURHOOD BUILDING BLOCKS

**CASE STUDIES**

- 'Mehr als Wohnen'
  and Kalkbreite,
  Zürich, Switzerland
- Fruitvale, Oakland,
  USA

- Poor living conditions and social isolation
  diminish the quality of our lives.
- Well-designed, well-managed buildings and
  public spaces generate a sense of security and
  ownership in local communities.
- The combination of mixed uses and dwellings
  creates a local focus and reference point for
  adjacent neighbourhoods.

*'The social life of cities, in particular the ordinary, the small-scale and mundane aspects of urban life, are commonly overlooked as a source of insight and inspiration for city planners and decision makers.'*

**SAFFRON WOODCRAFT**
*Social Life*[1]

## INTRODUCTION

A nascent community's choice to settle in a particular location will have been determined by the topographic and climatic qualities that made it suitable as a place for them to build their lives.

Settlements can have something of a Russian Doll quality; smaller ones nested inside larger ones. Walkable communities, of which there may be many within a town or city, occupy central positions within the larger, strategic scale of urban planning. By the same token there can be several neighbourhood building blocks within one walkable community.

Neighbourhood building blocks take the scale of planning to the finer grain that, without embarking on analysis of architecture, touches on aspects of built form and the design of smaller urban spaces.

## POOR LIVING CONDITIONS AND SOCIAL ISOLATION DIMINISH THE QUALITY OF OUR LIVES

Social isolation is an increasing issue in towns and cities. Despite being physically surrounded by many people in high population areas, paradoxically it can be more alienating due to a lack of intimate connection and community. *The Lancet* report of September 2016, 'City planning and population health: a global challenge', sets out how serious the effects of social isolation can be: 'A 2015 meta-analysis concluded that the impact of social isolation on premature mortality was comparable to other established health risk factors (eg, obesity), highlighting its importance as a public health issue.'[2]

Well-designed neighbourhoods establish the spatial frameworks that can help to avoid social isolation and nurture a good quality of life. The function of neighbourhood building blocks is at the local level where there is greatest scope for the creation of therapeutic, human-scale environments. To encourage people to congregate, places need to feel safe, be served by easily accessible social facilities and not affected by the impacts of traffic fumes and noise.

Residential layouts work best when organised along well-overlooked public streets, softened with street trees and with car parking designed to be as discrete as possible. This contributes to the creation of a sense of community based on a clear definition of public and private territory, including 1.5 m or more of 'defensible space'. This is the area between the back edge of the pavement and the front doors to houses and apartments. The design of such transitions between public and private space has evolved over time and has established recognised patterns for the planning of residential neighbourhoods.

This relates to front railings, gates and gardens, decorative porches and door surrounds, at least one entrance step and windows or peepholes that enabled residents to glimpse who was coming to the front door. Too many of these time-honoured measures were dismissed as Modernist ideas were explored, often leading to a lack of definition between the fronts and backs of blocks in residential developments. In many cases, often in areas of social housing, the spatial structure needed to be redesigned or even demolished when the housing proved to be unfit for purpose. Urbanists and placemakers generally recognise that the traditional urban block is the most reliable and flexible means of organising space, particularly for the design of residential accommodation.

Rear gardens of houses should be arranged back-to-back to maximise privacy and security. Plots located on street corners should maintain the continuity of street frontages for the same reasons. For apartments, the issue of the security of amenity space is blurred by the fact that it is shared by residents, not all of whom may know one another when there have been changes of occupancy. This makes it harder to distinguish genuine residents and visitors from intruders and means it is all the more important for these shared semi-private spaces to be clearly defined and well-overlooked.

Adherence to these criteria establishes a fundamental sense of order that promotes feelings of confidence and stability amongst residents, which in turn helps to build trust and a sense of belonging to a stable community. This can be a source of support for people with mental health problems for whom the design of individual homes, of whatever tenure, should strike an appropriate balance between feeling connected with what is going on in the public realm and having the privacy they need.

Loneliness can be ameliorated when the layout of homes encourages neighbours to drop-by on an informal basis, when appropriate, and when residents who may feel shy or vulnerable are tempted to join in with activities taking place amongst people with whom they feel comfortable and safe. The sensitivity of this type of situation is an example of where the transitional spaces, mentioned above, play a particularly valuable part.

Hunt Thompson Associates' Lea View House, a seminal and highly influential project for the London Borough of Hackney, completed in 1984, is an excellent example of how spatial organisation and community spirit can be

**FIGURE 3.3.1**
Lea View House – a block transformed

improved through tenant participation and imaginative, sensitive design. The descriptions provided are based on a combination of conversations with the project architects and content from *Community Architecture* by Nick Wates and Charles Knevitt, Routledge (first published by Routledge in 1987).

In this existing rectilinear urban block, all access to the apartments was from an internal, hard-landscaped courtyard used for car parking. The 'back garden' amenity space that faced outwards towards the street was inaccessible and therefore neglected, having no doors opening onto it from the ground floor flats and being cut off from the street by metal railings. In other words, the whole building block was inside out.

To address these multiple issues, the team adopted the pioneering approach of establishing a project office in a vacant flat as a means of maximising engagement with the residents of the 250 dwellings. The majority of them wanted to move out as the blocks were notorious for crime, vandalism and racial tension. Initial scepticism was overcome as the tenants became involved with the project's design from day one, and their detailed knowledge of how the block did or did not work was central to the design of the plans that were introduced. This was an indispensable learning process both for the residents and the architects.

The radical strategy that emerged was to reorganise the fronts and backs of the dwellings by creating traditional, ground floor street entrances with defensible front gardens that led to two-storey family homes. This was achieved by combining existing ground and first floor flats to become duplexes with new internal staircases leading to first floor rooms that overlooked the front and rear gardens. The tenure was diversified with smaller apartments on the upper three floors refurbished for young couples and elderly residents and served by new lift-towers accessed from separate street entrances, as shown in Figure 3.3.1.

With all dwellings accessed from the public street, the internal courtyard became a shared private green space, with a refurbished community building at the main street entrance space. The involvement of the residents strengthened community ties and generated a sense of ownership that improved the quality of their lives. Crime and vandalism were virtually eliminated after the renovation, common areas remained spotless and the improvements were shown to have health benefits including significant reductions in smoking, and physical and mental health problems.

This description of the Lea View House process also illustrates the value of community empowerment. Lea View House was a Community Architecture project where the participants were from the same building and generally shared the same goals. It is also a good example of how social diversity can develop. The existing blocks consisted of repetitive flat layouts but more variety was introduced when the bottom two floors were converted into family duplexes with gardens. Smaller apartments on the upper three floors benefited from the improved accessibility provided by the new lift towers and were more suited to young people, elderly residents and/or people with limited mobility. The overall reshaping of the blocks shows how social diversity and inclusivity can be generated to serve residents from a range of age-groups and stages in life, as reflected in their differing patterns of activity during the day.

## WELL-DESIGNED, WELL-MANAGED BUILDINGS AND PUBLIC SPACES GENERATE A SENSE OF SECURITY AND OWNERSHIP IN THE LOCAL COMMUNITY

In the 1970s William Whyte was a pioneer of urban life who instigated the 'Street Life Project' in New York City. Whyte's team noted the importance of seating areas, the role trees and foliage play in sheltering people from the elements, and the tendency of crowds to congregate around amenities such as food vendors. 'What attracts people most,' Whyte noted, 'is other people.'[3]

Whyte's work influenced the Danish urbanist Jan Gehl, and JTP benefited from working with some of Gehl's colleagues on a project in the Hanseatic League World Heritage Site in the city of Lübeck, Germany. The commission involved the local community in a participatory planning process to develop ideas to improve the public realm in the heart of the historic city centre, and a key outcome was the series of public space principles, consisting of the following eight criteria:

- safety and tranquillity
- a comfortable microclimate
- places to spend time
- visual connections
- enclosure and sense of place
- townscape qualities
- unique identity
- user-friendliness and accessibility.

The eight principles can be grouped together as integrated guidance for the creation of: user-friendly places with comfortable micro-climates where people are happy to spend time, whether safe and quiet or stimulating and lively, benefitting from clear spatial articulation and interesting visual connections whose townscape qualities create a strong sense of identity.

The team used these criteria to analyse seven of Lübeck's key urban spaces in terms of their existing layouts and the ways the team proposed to improve their spatial qualities. (It was this methodology that subsequently inspired the DAS system illustrated in Chapter 3.)

Safety and tranquillity

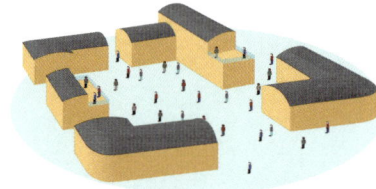

Spatial articulation

Comfortable micro-climate

Townscape qualities

Places to spend time

Identity

Visual connections

Ease of use

**FIGURE 3.3.2** Public space principles

The city's history revolved around seven urban quarters, each having its own space and church spire, and this was celebrated by local participants around a hands-on-planning table by naming their concept *'7 Türme, 7 Plätze = 7. Himmel'!* ('7 towers, 7 squares = 7th heaven'!) Each of these quarters can be seen as neighbourhood building blocks whose design can reflect the eight public space principles illustrated above.

## THE COMBINATION OF MIXED USES AND DWELLINGS CREATES A LOCAL FOCUS AND REFERENCE POINT FOR ADJACENT NEIGHBOURHOODS

For the regeneration of a former barracks in the German city of Tübingen to become a mixed-use neighbourhood, one of the planning regulations stipulated that no residential accommodation would be permitted in the ground floor spaces in the key buildings. Many development companies would regard this as a lost opportunity, but in terms of urbanism and healthy placemaking it is an excellent strategy.

Apartments with balconies and/or winter-gardens at first floor level and above work well, as they not only offer secure, private outdoor space and views but also provide natural surveillance onto the surrounding street scene that makes the public realm feel safer and more sociable. Ground level residential accommodation is less straightforward, as it can be awkward to design in terms of providing enough daylight and sunlight, and ensuring adequate privacy and security for residents. These private spaces at ground floor level can also have the negative effect of preventing the adjacent public realm from being genuinely public.

This is important because ground floor frontage in urban locations is intrinsically valuable, regardless of whether the right businesses happen to turn up when the space in question is first up for rent or sale. Once designated as residential accommodation it is unlikely to become available for any other use whereas, if it remains public, the streetscape remains 'open for business' and can be given a designation that allows for a range of potential use-classes and agreed rental levels. With apartments above there is scope for part of the ground floor to become a live-work space on which residents would have

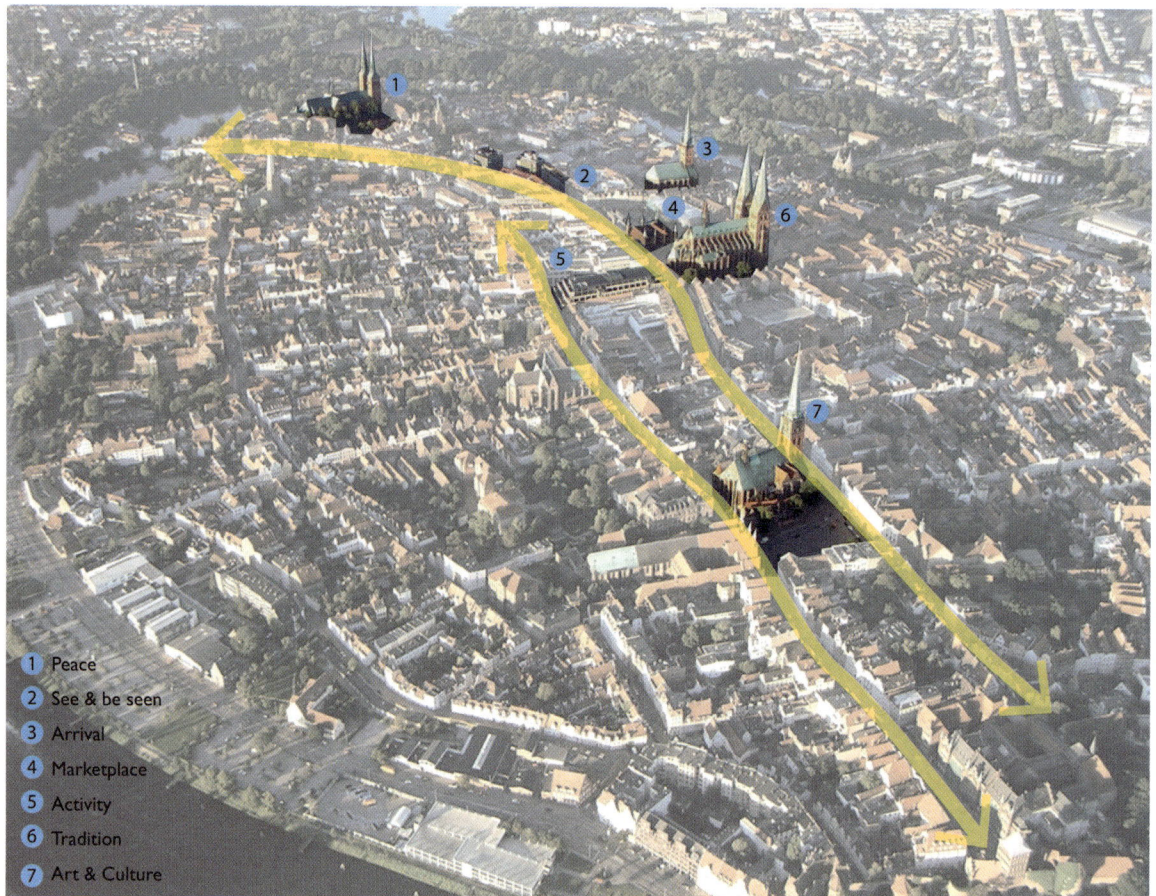

1  Peace
2  See & be seen
3  Arrival
4  Marketplace
5  Activity
6  Tradition
7  Art & Culture

**FIGURE 3.3.3**
Consensus masterplan,
'Seven towers, Seven squares
= Seventh heaven!'

first refusal before it is offered more widely. Or the occupants may decide to use it communally for residents' association meetings or classes based on the enthusiasms of special interest groups and youth activities.

The range of possible activities that can be accommodated at this local scale makes a valuable contribution to local identity and the building of neighbourhood networks that strengthen the social fabric of the settlement. With several of these distributed within a series of adjacent walkable communities, individual groups can become known for their particular interests and this can lead to new social connections. Kent and Thompson's report on 'Connecting and strengthening communities' points out that: 'Neighbourhood destinations also provide settings for cultural and informal social activities that can enhance community connections and sense of belonging.'[4] These qualities make a fundamental contribution to the health and wellbeing of individuals and communities.

# KEY LESSONS

### INDIVIDUAL AND COLLECTIVE WELLBEING
Neighbourhood building blocks generate health benefits by establishing places where people with interests and enthusiasms can meet and exchange ideas. This should also encourage social diversity and inclusivity which help to broaden people's networks and strengthen community cohesion.

### ADDRESSING LONELINESS AND ISOLATION
Social cohesion and enthusiasm at a local level are important for everyone, and in particular for those in need of support due to age or mental frailty. Social interaction helps people make new contacts, learn new skills, develop hobbies and enjoy leisure activities.

### BUILDING CONFIDENCE AND A SENSE OF SECURITY
To minimise fear of crime and encourage sociability, houses and flats must be well-planned and streets and public spaces must feel friendly and safe.

### HOW TO REALISE THESE QUALITIES BY DESIGN?
- Provide well-managed buildings that include facilities where local residents can meet to make shared decisions, learn new skills, develop hobbies and enjoy leisure activities.
- Provide well-designed houses and flats constructed from sustainable, healthy materials.
- Create spatial layouts for houses with clear definitions between public and private space: defensible, semi-private spaces facing the street; private,

back to back garden areas to the rear; and clear, secure arrangements on corners at the ends of terraces.

- Apartment buildings should be lined at ground floor level with mixed-use, active frontages onto public streets, complemented by inviting, outdoor spaces that encourage social interaction and communal activity.
- Ensure there are 'eyes on the street' from houses and apartments that overlook the public realm to generate a sense of safety and discourage crime.
- Access to apartment buildings must be designed for security, with higher level balconies, winter gardens and roof terraces to provide residential amenity and natural surveillance onto streets.
- Create environments that encourage social diversity and inclusivity.
- Create well-designed public spaces providing: safety and tranquillity; a comfortable micro-climate; places to spend time; visual connections; enclosure and sense of place; townscape qualities; unique identity; user-friendliness and accessibility.

CASE STUDY 3.3.1

# 'MEHR ALS WOHNEN', HUNZIGER AREAL AND KALKBREITE, ZÜRICH, SWITZERLAND

**FIGURE 3.3.4**
Hunziger Areal – varied typologies and relaxed green space

## 1. 'MEHR ALS WOHNEN'

Constructed on a former cement works, the Hunziger Areal in the north of Zürich is a housing cooperative created by a group of entrepreneurs. Switzerland has a history of cooperative housing and the title 'Mehr als Wohnen' ('more than living') expresses their vision of life in a communal environment, supported by their membership and embodying progressive, social and political values. It has a primary school built on several floors to allow for more green space and the accommodation consists of 373 dwellings in mid-rise blocks including studios, apartments and cluster flats. Rents are calculated on a cost-rent basis and 20% of units are subsidised to allow for those living on welfare benefits.

**FIGURE 3.3.5** Hunziger Areal – ground floor mixed uses include a bike pool and bike store

**FIGURE 3.3.6** Hunziger Areal – community garden and multi-storey school

## A COMMUNITY BASED ON SHARING

The ethos of 'Mehr als Wohnen' is the establishment of a supportive, sharing community, with thoughtfully laid-out internal and external spaces, nurtured by a committed management organisation. This bodes well for the maintenance of good levels of social interaction, inclusivity and the avoidance of feelings of loneliness and isolation. The development incorporates an impressively wide range of housing typologies. Perhaps the most innovative is cluster-flat housing in which the dwellings are designed with private bed and bathroom areas but shared communal spaces for cooking, eating and living. A nearby data centre generates large amounts of excess energy which is piped into the residential development to heat the dwellings.

There is no residents' car parking within the scheme but a basement with 106 bays provides space for business vehicles and a car sharing scheme. The communal approach includes ground-floor space for small businesses and communal activities, well-equipped, shared laundry rooms, a bike pool and a bike store. Ground floor mixed-uses also include a psychology practice, a kindergarten, remedial education, a painting studio and occupational therapy workshop, music, dance and yoga studios, a hairdressing salon, a bakery and a restaurant.

Well-proportioned and well-overlooked communal outdoor spaces consist of hard- and soft-landscaping which have a relaxed, unmanicured feel. This results from a collective

**FIGURE 3.3.7** Kalkbreite – entrance stairs rising up to shared terrace from street

decision made by the residents to allow themselves time to work out how best to use the spaces. At ground level is a productive, community garden, and at high level in a central block is a well-appointed sauna facility with a roof garden above it that offers views across Zürich and to the Alps.

## AREAS FOR IMPROVEMENT

The school was in itself unduly expensive but, having several storeys, the building's footprint must be smaller, perhaps allowing more space for other uses including residential accommodation and amenity space?

## 2. KALKBREITE

Kalkbreite is a highly innovative, new housing cooperative close to Zürich's city centre, built next to a railway line and over a still-functioning tram depot. The 97 dwelling development is designed with a mix of sizes and tenures, and the cooperative has a membership of 1,500 that is made possible by a Swiss system that allows investment to be provided at attractive rates.

Addressing the street at ground floor level are a series of mixed uses occupying 20% of the overall built area of the project. These include a cinema, shops, a medical practice and a restaurant with outdoor seating and, internally, a plate glass window through which one can observe the parked trams. The active frontages make a continuous line of ground floor uses that generate a lively street

**FIGURE 3.3.8** Kalkbreite – multi-functional communal terrace above tram depot

**FIGURE 3.3.9** Kalkbreite – healthily challenging exercise workout

environment, helping to overcome the challenging constraints of its triangular site, shoe-horned between a railway line and three busy roads.

The residential element sits above the tram depot, and is reached by a stylish, open stairway, leading up to a large, semi-private, south-west facing courtyard terrace overlooked by the apartments. Its landscape design includes a variety of different spaces to suit residents of all ages including raised planting beds, seating areas and play equipment. Considerable thought and imagination seem to have been applied to create a diverse and inclusive community.

## AREAS FOR IMPROVEMENT
This is a very difficult site and the way the multiple constraints have been overcome to create a high quality, mixed-use, residential environment deserves praise, so it seems inappropriate to look for ways it could be improved.

# CASE STUDY 3.3.2
# FRUITVALE, OAKLAND, USA

**FIGURE 3.3.10**
Fruitvale – market stalls at exit
from BART Station

Oakland is inventive in finding ways to establish an identity independent of its more fashionable neighbour, San Francisco, across the Bay Bridge.

Researchers from UCLA's Latino Policy and Politics Initiative report that this 'transit village' has been a boon to the surrounding neighbourhood without resulting in gentrification. There are concerns that many low-income and working-class residents across the state are forced to leave urban areas due to rising rents and home prices. But the UCLA researchers have seen Oakland's Fruitvale neighbourhood holding onto its existing residents, along with its signature Mexican-American culture.

**FIGURE 3.3.11** Fruitvale – the central mixed-use square is a sociable meeting space

**FIGURE 3.3.12** Fruitvale – apartments overlooking public spaces bring a sense of community

**FIGURE 3.3.13** Fruitvale – gateway marking the transition from public square to busy street

## MIXED USES AT A TRANSIT STOP

Fruitvale is a Transit-orientated Development (TOD) situated next to the BART (Bay Area Rapid Transit) stop that shares its name, occupied by a mainly Latino population. The primary public space consists of low-rise apartments over ground floor mixed-uses that accommodate market traders, shops, eateries and community services. The Fruitvale Public Market is a second focus with a sociable atmosphere and places serving food from a variety of ethnic origins.

These facilities are accessed from lively public spaces, decked-out with colour, and generating a strong sense of community. The central areas near the BART station feel comfortable and seem to be well-suited to the local residents and traders. The combination of entrances to the upper floor apartments interspersed with the varied mix of uses creates an intimate, convivial atmosphere.

It is impressive to see how the Fruitvale transit stop that is located in a low to middle income neighbourhood has been fertile ground for this community to carve out its own unique identity.

**FIGURE 3.3.14** Fruitvale Public Market, a popular place to meet and eat

**FIGURE 3.3.15** Fruitvale – adjacent street that would benefit from upgrade

## AREAS FOR IMPROVEMENT

A reasonable proposal to extend pedestrian priority within the public realm through the closure to traffic of a quiet, internal street is also under consideration.

There is potential for the lively nucleus established around the transit stop to be extended, to improve the less-developed areas nearby.

# CHAPTER 3.4
# MOVEMENT NETWORKS

**CASE STUDIES**
- Berliner Platz, Essen, Germany
- Oklahoma City, USA

- People in cars tend to think traffic is caused by other people.
- Providing many options for sustainable 'active travel' makes getting about safer and quicker, providing exercise in daily life; breathing cleaner air.
- Accidents involving cars travelling at less than 20 mph are considerably less likely to end in fatalities. The '20's Plenty!' concept is particularly relevant for mixed-use neighbourhoods.

*'Never in human history have people moved their bodies around the world so much without moving their bodies.'*

**DAVID PENCHEON**[1]

## INTRODUCTION

We are faced by a future characterised either by ever-increasing volumes of traffic and tarmac, or developing sustainable, responsible, equitable and healthy movement strategies by using the same level of ingenuity as created motorised vehicles in the first place.

Technological innovations to reduce the air pollution and carbon emissions caused by motor vehicles address some of the problems of getting about but, from the perspective of healthy placemaking, they leave others untouched. As mentioned earlier, even non-fossil fuel, energy-efficient vehicles emit Type 2.5 particulate patter (PM 2.5), the microscopic, toxic dust caused by brakes, car tyres and the road surface itself. When inhaled, these remain in our bodies and contribute to respiratory and other illnesses, so travelling more slowly would at least reduce the amounts of PM 2.5 emitted.

Research and development are needed to reduce the risks, but even if the PM 2.5 issues were overcome, the vehicles nonetheless constitute an inefficient use of urban space, both when in motion and parked, thereby monopolising valuable land that could be allocated more equitably to other uses.

People need to travel and the growing pressure for people to reduce car use suggests an increase in the various forms of active travel. This corresponds to the WHO's report stating that: 'The new WHO global action plan to promote physical activity responds to the requests by countries for updated guidance, and a framework of effective and feasible policy actions to increase physical activity at all levels.'[2]

## PARKING REFORMS

To create walkable communities, the space allocated to vehicle movement and parking should be minimised to allow the urban structure to be compact. Discouraging parking is the answer and several strategies exist to achieve this. Parking charges have been in force for decades and road-pricing in urban centres has been introduced more recently, despite the political challenges this faces. The most stringent approach is to prohibit public parking altogether in urban centres, other than for people with limited mobility.

Our movement networks need to be improved to make them work in a more economical and equitable way. The principles set out in this book propose reforms that may be seen as threats to patterns of behaviour that have evolved in society over many decades. But the reasons for proposing them are all directed towards improving public health, and the scientific, sociological and medical evidence documenting the need for these changes is consistent across the professional spectrum. To resist or dismiss proposals for change shows a lack of concern for the health of all citizens.

Large tracts of urban space in settlements of all sizes are allocated to parking, which goes hand in hand with having a limited public transport system. Car parks are mono-functional areas of paving, sometimes on many floors, devoid of the stimulating qualities of other uses that characterise good urban environments. Walking past them is uninteresting; something the motorists themselves experience when they get out of their cars and shape-shift to become pedestrians. To reach their chosen destinations on foot they then negotiate the parked cars left by all who arrived with the same intentions, and must cross the roads that enabled their vehicles to convey them to their parking spaces.

Areas of town centre parking fragment urban layouts, as can be seen in Figure 3.4.1, that shows a diagram of Newbury in West Berkshire. Newbury is a market town with a population of circa 50,000 that has allocated large areas in the town centre to car parking; at grade and in multi-storey structures.

The town is located on a railway line with fast trains to London and provides parking for commuters and also for shoppers and people working in the town centre. The amount of car parking between the town centre and the station makes walking from one to the other circuitous and devoid of interest. Although Newbury gains revenue from the parking fees, in terms of land use the combination of the car parking itself and the traffic generated by those driving into the town to reach it seems uneconomical. Newbury has been working on plans to address the situation, but the layout shown on Figure 3.4.1 gives a sense how much space could be made available if much of the parking were to be curtailed. With fewer cars trying to access the town centre, traffic would be limited mainly to buses, taxis, commercial and emergency vehicles, making the environment for pedestrians more agreeable.

Any study to explore these ideas would of course require agreement at town and county level, and fervent opposition from car users and retailers would be inevitable. But it would in principle be possible to analyse how the overall pattern of traffic movements could be upgraded in response to 21st-century needs. If health considerations were to be prioritised, air quality, road safety, reduced traffic congestion and the multiple benefits of active travel would be the most compelling arguments, along with the opportunities to re-purpose the newly available urban space for new uses. Newbury is far from unique, as countless other settlements allocate comparable amounts of valuable space to parking.

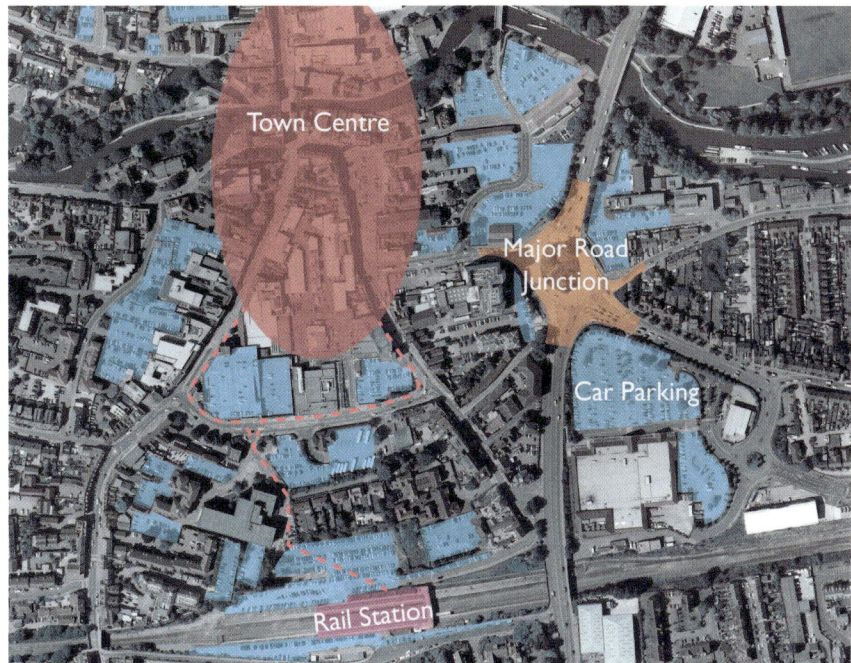

**FIGURE 3.4.1**
Space occupied by parking (shown in blue) in Newbury town centre

# PEOPLE IN CARS TEND TO THINK TRAFFIC IS CAUSED BY OTHER PEOPLE

### HOW SHOULD WE GET ABOUT?

Transport is operated by professional drivers of public transport services, business vehicles and by private owners.

Aeroplanes, railways and underground trains use their dedicated and highly efficient routes and are driven by professionals. For travellers to access the places they have come to visit involves a change of transport mode. Trams, buses and taxis provide this service and operate in the public realm along with professional drivers of ambulances, fire engines, refuse vehicles, delivery lorries and vans, for whom it is their full-time job.

Into this mixture of professionalism, where the job itself depends on their driving responsibly, come the owners of private vehicles for whom being penalised for irresponsible driving is an irritation but is unlikely to be a threat to their employment.

This combination of drivers of private vehicles and professional road users generates many areas for friction and potential conflict, amongst which pedestrians and the users of motorcycles, mopeds and bicycles are not only the least land-hungry but also the most physically vulnerable.

Many of the world's cities have allowed the public realm to become a free-for-all whose consequences are detrimental both to citizens' physical and mental health and the cities' economic prosperity. A free-for-all in the context of a settlement, large or small, will not work. The sheer complexity of our activities means they must be organised to function effectively, and our health is amongst the most important criteria to embed in its planning. Jan Gehl expressed this idea, saying: 'One thing is clear, healthy cities don't just happen – they are built on purpose. When we don't just consider health a personal issue, we open our eyes to the health potential in the spaces we share. We could open up more outdoors classes for school children, and more walking meetings for the workforce. If we make active transportation a priority, we would build cities that make it easy to walk and bike around and thereby reduce commuting by car.'[3]

## THE NATURAL SELECTION OF STREETS

The public thoroughfare is a structure that dates back to humankind's earliest habitations; an instantly recognisable feature in settlements everywhere that has continued to function in the same basic way as it always did. Built form defines linear spaces to provide pedestrian and vehicular access to the public and/or private uses that the buildings contain. The thoroughfare, or street, also functions as a movement corridor to more distant destinations.

When a street's only users are pedestrians, the broad range of circulation and social interaction can go on easily, as we all operate at a human scale. Add the greater speed and strength of vehicles and new challenges present themselves for which we cannot claim to have found a permanent, equitable formula, despite millennia of trying.

The vehicles' greater speed and strength are undeniable advantages for the transport of goods and people, but can also be socially divisive, lead to accidents and cause pollution. Due to their advantages, vehicles have been designated a large share of road space, whilst pedestrians have been deprioritised. This must change, and there are encouraging signs that it will, but we need to pressurise decision-makers to expedite the process. For instance, our Highway Code still emphasises the dangers of motor vehicles in their warnings to pedestrians about how to cross roads. This implies that roads are dangerous to use, a concern that is further exacerbated by some drivers' propensity to break speed limits.

## SIZE AND SPEED

Most urban space is public, and the private car has been permitted to occupy it, generally unopposed. The reason the balance tends to work to the detriment of pedestrians is a question of scale.

### WHEN STATIONARY

People occupy approximately: 1 m²; cycles: 2 m²; cars – allowing for manoeuvring space – when parallel parked: c. 10-12 m²; and right-angled: 20 m².

### WHEN IN MOTION

Walking: 0-4 mph; cycling: 0-15 mph or more; driving: 0-60 mph or more.

The limits of the speeds that can be achieved and the amounts that can be carried by pedestrians and cyclists cannot compare with those of cars, which can reach 60 mph in 5 seconds, carrying in comfort four or more passengers, and their luggage, for hundreds of miles. This makes them exceptionally useful on motorways which are monofunctional, mechanistic systems that have more in common with railways than urban streets. Between these poles are the 'A' and 'B' roads that connect settlements, for which the appropriate balance of uses is hard to determine.

**WIDTH**

Pedestrians: 60 cm; bicycles: 60 cm; cars: 1.6–2.0 m or more.

On a street, each car occupies three times the width and over twice the length of a cyclist, five times that of a pedestrian and is far less manoeuvrable. Pedestrians can turn on the spot and a dismounted bicycle can be turned in its own length. Both are very flexible in negotiating urban spaces whilst vehicles require much more room, whether in motion, stationary in traffic, or parked.

Taken together, these bald statistics add up to a series of impacts. Private motor vehicles take up a disproportionate amount of space, distorting the way the public realm can be used and marginalising pedestrians and cyclists whose flexibility and agility are what enable busy urban spaces to function. A more compact, human-scale atmosphere is generated when moving or parked vehicles no longer dominate the urban street scene. The active travel this involves means that public transport, including taxis, will still be present, along with emergency vehicles and controlled delivery and business traffic.

## ATTITUDES TO MOBILITY

Large cities can only function if enough of us make use of the opportunities for active travel, but in many smaller cities and towns the balance of those factors is often too much in favour of private vehicles. These settlement centres are likely to be destinations for people who live in outlying villages, as is the case with places such as Newbury, and take it for granted that they can park in the centre where they may monopolise the available public space. The attractiveness and functionality even of small village squares can end up being deprived of their former, social purposes by poorly-organised vehicle movement and parking arrangements.

Running participatory planning workshops for the design of new neighbourhoods or settlement extensions shows there is a primary reason why existing residents oppose the idea. Particularly in the UK, it seems they believe that additional traffic congestion will be caused if the population in their locality is increased. The irony is that it is often the residents who have moved in most recently who object the most. The main justifications for their opposition are:

a) The traffic is already awful, and more residents will just make it worse.

b) The public transport service is slow, unreliable and infrequent.

c) The traffic congestion is a nightmare and is worse in our area than anywhere else.

These attitudes are much less prevalent in an urban context where there are already enough people to support good public transport services and car dependency is low. This is either because residents rarely use the one they own, due to the availability of many other ways of getting about, or because they realise they are better-off without having one at all. Cities function this way but, for many smaller cities, towns and villages, the private car holds sway and traffic congestion is an apparently unavoidable, daily grind.

The theorist's response to the concerns of the local residents, best not expressed in public meetings, is:

1. All communities maintain that the traffic is worst in their area.

2. That is why we need to overcome congestion at a strategic level.

3. The local community's objections are interrelated because public transport could be faster, more reliable and more frequent if residents left their cars at home and travelled by bus, tram or chose to cycle.

4. Additional residents will increase demand for public transport, leading to an improved service for all.

5. The cost of housing nationally is far too high due to the shortage of supply which is why we need to build more homes, and they have to be located somewhere.

Even when residents accept the logic of these principles, their immediate needs take precedence, and the theorists themselves will accept that it will not happen quickly and a transition period would be necessary. Understandably, residents would prefer the existing problems they know rather than unknown new ones to come. Local authority transport planners find themselves in an unenviable position in the midst of these polarised opinions, most likely believing in the long-term strategic approach but too busy dealing with current traffic problems to implement it.

## OVERCOMING THE DILEMMA

So how can we address this? That the traffic is already a prominent issue is unlikely to persuade objectors to change their daily routines to accommodate newcomers. And even if sufficient numbers were to forsake the car as a means of reducing congestion, would not others simply take the opportunity to re-colonise the newly available road space liberated by their generosity?

In the face of complicated situations such as these, we can mobilise four basic strategies:

### 1. CARROT AND STICK (AND ITS CLOSE RELATIVE 'NO CRITICISM WITHOUT RECOMMENDATION')

The key factor is that if the 'stick' involves asking people to change how they travel, they need to be offered the 'carrot' of an enticing alternative; and one that really works. Experience shows that providing the carrot but no stick means they will not change.

But it is the carrot plus stick that has transformed places like Copenhagen and Freiburg into the healthy places they are; a result of what the proposed changes are and the way they are presented. This involves the road being reorganised with increased space for active travel and a reduction of that for private cars.

### 2. THE NUDGE AND/OR STEALTH

The adaptation of our movement networks to rebalance the way we allocate urban space may need authorisation from the top but can also be initiated at grassroots level. This involves a stealthier approach that effects change gradually so it is scarcely noticed until its positive effects have been assimilated into everyday life.

### 3. FROM THE TOP

Major changes on how we get about are always contentious and, even when approved, will require meticulous planning to manage the transition phase. The Congestion Charge seems to suit central London because many of its historic streets are quite narrow, whereas in younger cities, with streets designed to accommodate large volumes of traffic, a congestion charge may be less appropriate.

As the benefits of these transformations of the public realm become apparent, the 'nudge' proposals become easier to introduce, with moves such as narrowing streets and widening pavements, as has been done in many cities including Portland, Oregon and Warsaw and is described in more detail later in this chapter.

Ben Page of Ipsos MORI UK pointed out that had a referendum been held on introducing the Congestion Charge in London the vote would have gone against the idea. Despite some problems, the overall consensus on the Congestion Charge is that it has improved Central London's movement network, which reminds us that voting, or other forms of consultation to resolve complex issues, does not always produce the best outcomes. As a well-balanced opinion from *The Conversation* points out: 'After 15 years of operation, London's Congestion Charge can be celebrated as a success. It has set the bar for other cities – demonstrating that road pricing can only be successful as part of strategy that offers efficient, sustainable alternatives for car drivers. Looking ahead, the Congestion Charge needs reform to meet the financial and logistical challenge of providing a good transport system for Londoners.'[4] It is encouraging that Stockholm and Singapore already have such charges and New York City will be the first in the USA, in 2021, with other US cities considering the idea.

## 4. ECONOMIC REALITY

Cars are expensive to buy, tax, insure, maintain and fill up with fuel, and their value depreciates fast, particularly when bought new. But it is an investment that, once made, gives people freedom to go where they want when they want, so it makes sense to use it for all journeys rather than spending additional outlay on public transport as well.

Were they to calculate the cost of that investment in advance and work out how many taxi rides or car rental journeys it would buy, it would at least give them pause for thought. That said, for most people, the convenience, satisfaction and status that come with car ownership, particularly when the cars are parked right next to the house, outweigh these rational arguments, whilst the equally rational list of individual and collective health risks falls by the wayside. An additional compelling factor is the technical virtuosity of modern motor vehicles which many people find irresistible.

Economic reality also relates to land value, and the amount of space the two or three cars occupy when parked on a newly-built residential plot can only increase the purchase price of the dwellings. Development companies recognise that sites could accommodate more dwellings if less of the area were allocated to car parking. The reasons they tend not to do so are:

- Experience tells them they will not be able to sell dwellings whose space for car parking is constrained.
- Local authorities require them to provide enough spaces to avert the concerns of neighbours fearing that too few spaces in the new development would cause over-spill onto the streets near to where they live.

This scenario in which the private cars take up what can be seen as a disproportionate amount of site area is most evident in suburban developments. Low-density family housing tends to be particularly land-hungry. Whilst the space the parked cars occupy has increased with the number allocated per dwelling and the size of the vehicles themselves, the size of gardens has reduced. The reasoning may be that people are too busy to look after them, and the smaller garden offsets the increase in purchase price caused by more cars on plot. From the point of view of high quality placemaking, the large amounts of space taken up by cars parked next to dwellings represent a significant challenge.

But the limited plot sizes that result in an apparent lack of green space compared to hardstanding does have a positive aspect, in erring towards a healthier residential density. This greenery deficit can itself be offset if/when owners decide to have fewer cars than the developers felt they had to allow for and can simply re-purpose the space gained into garden areas. Another technique is to pre-empt fewer cars by positioning the second or third space in the garden and leaving it to the owner to decide where their priorities lie, as applied in Poundbury, Dorset.

Parking standards for low-density apartment buildings typically see a sizeable proportion of their site area taken up by car parks, sometimes at the expense of amenity space. Developers recoil at the cost of below-ground car parking, but as densities increase in more urban contexts a point is reached when it becomes economically viable. The outcome is that with parked cars below ground, more and higher-quality amenity space and public realm is possible.

These points relate to the existing situation in most developed countries in terms of the role cars play in our lives, but there is evidence that car use is in decline. This tendency is a result both of changing attitudes in younger generations and the increasing promotion of new mobility concepts. These include 'Connected Autonomous Vehicles' (CAVs) and 'Mobility As A Service' (MAAS), accompanied by the suggestion that car ownership may shrink in favour of our use of a car or taxi as and when we need it. The statistic being widely circulated to support this idea is that the cars we own are stationary 95% of the time and can therefore be seen as profligate expenditures of space and money.

## TAKING ADVANTAGE OF THE MANY OPTIONS FOR SUSTAINABLE 'ACTIVE TRAVEL' MAKES GETTING ABOUT SAFER, QUICKER AND HEALTHIER

The recent proliferation of the options we now have for getting about is welcome, as it offers alternatives to what was previously a limited choice. Adjustments are being made to the way the public realm is shared, with cities in many countries rebalancing the space allocated to vehicles to allow more for pedestrians and cyclists. Whether large or small, these interventions, if well designed and executed, all contribute to the humanising and human-scaling of our urban environments.

The tactics of turning car spaces into bike spaces, or an area of restaurant seating, is a clever way to bring about change, and can also include economic benefits. An example of this is described in Living Streets' 'Pedestrian Pound': 'Small-scale improvements to the pedestrian environment also offer evidence of increased spending. In June 2017, a temporary "parklet" in Shoreditch, East London – which turned a space normally occupied by two cars into seating for 14 people and 8 cycle parking spaces – increased the adjacent shops takings by 20%.'[5]

This process is known as 'Road Space Reallocation' and involves adapting road space currently devoted to vehicle traffic or parking to serve other modes. This may be to widen pavements, introduce bicycle lanes and bike-parking spaces, and plant street trees. Beyond adaptation for transport related uses, larger areas can be used to create interesting and productive environments such as roadside extensions for food and drink outlets, public spaces animated by artwork, green space, new social facilities, business premises or housing. Figure 3.4.2, of a street in Warsaw, Poland, shows how pleasant a street can be when the pavement has been widened and the road space reduced. Street furniture demarcates the different uses of space and thoughtful paving, rather than tarmac, has been used as an additional way of creating a human-scale atmosphere.

The growing realisation that the economic value of urban space increases hand-in-hand with its social value is why we recognise that the space per person occupied by the movement and parking of private vehicles is disproportionately large compared with that of the many preferred modes categorised as 'active travel'.

The Living Streets document 'The Pedestrian Pound' refers to a document produced by Turner et al which reinforces this point: 'Improvements to the pedestrian environment are also associated with increased footfall. Turner et al (2011) conducted a before-and-after study of new or improved facilities in eight New Zealand cities known to create difficulties for pedestrians. These included the provision of kerb extensions and refuge islands and controlled crossings. Pedestrian use increased in seven of the eight sites, ranging from 7% to 90%.'[6]

## IMPROVING MOVEMENT SYSTEMS

Forward-thinking governments and local authorities fund initiatives encouraging people to engage in active travel, having understood that the money will have been well-spent. In creating a high quality system, the focus of the provisions needs to involve not only the physical design decisions that serve the numerous ways of getting about but also an emphasis on high quality communication and real-time information to give travellers confidence that their journey is safe and going according to plan.

Jeff Tumlin of Nelson Nygaard got to the essence of movement networks, saying that 'The best transportation plan is a good land use plan.'[7] In other words, if the places people need to access are located and grouped together conveniently then the movement network can be efficient to use and economical to run. It is an approach that has much in common with the 'city of short distances' introduced in Chapter 2, and illustrated in Figure 3.1.3 in Chapter 3.

Movement networks need to be integrated into the layout of settlements and be easy for passengers to use across all transport modes. The increasing awareness of the benefits of healthy urban transport modes is spreading across many cities. Their planning and delivery is a complex process, but encouraging trends indicate that, albeit belatedly, active travel is being prioritised very widely. Systems are being modified to suit changing circumstances and the gradual reallocation of road space and parking areas in favour of less land-hungry ways of getting about is improving the quality of urban spaces. This creates new opportunities that designers will welcome.

Street networks follow the built form at ground level whilst the underground systems in major cities have the freedom to tunnel underneath urban blocks from one station to another; an ideal arrangement given the length and turning radii of the trains. Whether at grade or below ground, each settlement will have its own unique topography, geology and water systems of which the movement network needs to take account in determining optimal routes.

The main options for urban transport are buses, trams, light-rail, underground systems and, regardless of the items selected from this menu, the system must provide comprehensive, multi-modal networks laid out so that all residences are within 10 minutes' walk of a stop. Many cities combine local trains with faster ones with fewer stops to spread the ridership efficiently, of which the RER in Paris is an example.

To encourage passengers to use the system, changing between services and modes needs to be as smooth as possible, with carefully-planned interchanges, and should include urban transport systems accessing mainline trains and airports. Travel passes or other payment methods that enable movement between different modes make the experience simple and fast, and the regularity and frequency of service inspires users that the service will fulfil their expectations for journeys. Accurate, real-time information about vehicle timings at metro, bus and tram stops make the passengers' experience significantly easier when making choices about which routes and transport modes to use and is now facilitated by the proliferation of transport apps. Management of peak hour traffic is one of the biggest challenges for operators, and passengers, to overcome.

Clear signage and intelligible announcements at metro stations, multi-lingual as appropriate, assist orientation, and access through turnstiles is made easier when staff are available to assist passengers. Intelligible plans, maps and leaflets providing details of routes and places of local interest are important and all vehicles must be environmentally clean.

Whilst wealthy cities tend to have the best public transport systems, even places with access to very limited resources can aspire to make significant improvements to improve the quality of their transport networks, as shown in Curitiba, Brazil.

Curitiba, a city of around 2 million inhabitants, is celebrated for the work of former Mayor Jaime Lerner who in 1974 introduced a pioneering Bus Rapid Transit (BRT). It was the first in Brazil and its success inspired the implementation of similar plans in more than 100 cities around the world.

Earlier plans from 1943 had targeted an underground system whose costs prohibited its construction, whereas the above-ground BRT proved to be far cheaper to build and simpler to use, due to its visibility. The system's success was also a result of its being integrated with land use planning. This was based on a transect that encouraged high-density development along the BRT arteries, tapering down to lower density neighbourhoods further from the BRT and the city centre.

The popularity of Curitiba's BRT caused modal shift from automobile to bus travel. Based on 1991 traveller survey results, the BRT reduced auto trips by circa 27 million per year. 28% of BRT riders previously travelled by car, leading to one of the lowest rates of ambient air pollution in the country for cities of comparable size. In 2006 the system served over 1.3 million passengers, 80% using the express or direct bus services and spending about 10% of their income on travel – well below the national average.[8]

## HEALTHY MOBILITY

Increasing choice of mobility options reflects growing ingenuity in finding ways to adapt behaviour to an environment that is shared with other citizens, and these ideas mean that the private car can become less of a default option.

Buses, taxis, trams and over-ground and under-ground trains are the obvious choices and are classified as 'active' because of the energy we expend in getting to them, as is also the case with car sharing schemes and street cars. Getting daily exercise from walking, cycling, skateboarding and various types of scooter can be part of a healthy lifestyle, and the use of motorbikes, mopeds, electric bikes and electric scooters qualify as active travel because, although they are powered by engines, to use them involves physical exertion to some degree.

Cycling increases the distances people can access and saves time. Being very manoeuvrable, and occupying little space whether ridden, pushed or parked, riders are attracted by the convenience of dismounting within yards of their intended destinations. Surveys show that whilst cycling offers the advantages of being healthy, economical, enjoyable and environmentally friendly, the primary reason people cycle is that it is the quickest way to get about in urban environments, particularly when the minimal time, minimal amount of space and zero cost needed to find somewhere to park is taken into account.

Both walking and cycling are sociable, as people can make eye-contact with fellow citizens, smile or apologise as appropriate and stop for a chat without blocking the traffic. Cycling in many cities has an only partially-deserved reputation for being contentious, seen as being an irritant both to vehicle users and pedestrians. Cities with tram systems can be hazardous for cyclists, due to the dangers of the wheels becoming trapped in the lines. This can be overcome when the rails are designed to be continuous with the road surface.

Without going into the minefield of opinion this generates, it is interesting that some transport experts think the answer is to have segregated routes for cyclists whilst others believe it is the drivers and pedestrians who need to become more aware of cyclists.

From the point of view of healthy placemaking, cycling is a form of transport as valid as any other on our streets and, apart from walking, is not only by far the cleanest, healthiest and lowest-impact mode but can convey us more quickly and over longer distances than is possible with the equally valid option of getting about on foot.

## ACCIDENTS INVOLVING CARS TRAVELLING AT LESS THAN 20 MPH ARE CONSIDERABLY LESS LIKELY TO END IN FATALITIES. SO THE '20'S PLENTY!' CONCEPT IS PARTICULARLY RELEVANT FOR MIXED-USE NEIGHBOURHOODS

### CHANGE OF EMPHASIS

Nearly a century of vehicular domination has conditioned drivers, and to some extent pedestrians, to believe that the purpose of streets is to be linear, engineered spaces for vehicles to travel along, and that crossing them is dangerous.

The original function of that same street, whilst its linear quality remains important, is the desire both to walk across from pavement to pavement and to have the opportunity to occupy the centre of the space, currently only possible on a 'pedestrian refuge'.

Pedestrians have for decades been 'protected' from vehicles by railings and barriers whose effect is to pen them in like sheep, with the vehicles preventing them from going where they want to go. Many are still in place, but there are also good examples where they have been removed, for instance, at Oxford Circus and in Camden Town in London, both inspired by Japanese precedents.

Research in 2017 by Richard Mazuch and David McKenna showed that at 70 junctions in the road network, after the removal of guardrails there was 'a fall of 56% (43 to 19) in the number of collisions involving pedestrians who were killed or seriously injured'.[9] The Glasgow organisation 'Free Wheel North' is a charity taking a holistic view 'which works to remove barriers which prevent human-powered transport, be the barrier physical, a lack of knowledge, a lack of confidence, a lack of safe space or a lack of suitable equipment for those with mobility impairments'.[10]

Motor vehicles are the primary cause of road accidents and the speed at which they travel is a decisive factor. The Highway Code sets out the speeds that are suitable in different contexts, and road signs, speed humps and cameras aim to keep drivers in check. But the interesting work of Ben Hamilton-Baillie, the UK's most influential and innovative voice promoting the idea of 'shared space', adopted a different approach that taps into people's direct experience of the environment they are in, using psychological cues to get us to drive at the desired speed, with no need for speed humps or cameras.

As the term 'shared space' can polarise opinion with regard to the concerns of blind people, Hamilton-Baillie explored ways of using materials and spatial cues to reduce speeds and make streets safer for all, including those with visual impairments.

This involved designing roads that are safe, not because of intermittent speed humps, pedestrian refuges or chicanes, but because they are designed to get people driving more slowly of their own volition. It is achieved by using

**FIGURE 3.4.3** Shared space, Mariahilfer Strasse, Vienna – a busy arterial street closed to vehicles

**FIGURE 3.4.4** Shared space, Grassmarket, Edinburgh – a relaxing urban square

a combination of measures to lay out carriageways, such as arranging paving materials to make roads feel narrower than they are, as a means of bringing out the human in us. Strategically-located trees and street furniture combined with other visual effects function as subtle ways of shifting the responsibility for safe driving onto the drivers, rather than setting up a series of speed limits that too many people seem to believe were made to be broken.

Shared space continues to be adopted as a more harmonious way for different forms of mobility to interact, and a feature that can help to accommodate this is the variation of traffic intensity during the day. Closing streets to vehicles in the evening and during weekends can offer a welcome sense of freedom, humanised further when good quality paving is used to blur the distinction between road and pavement.

These ideas are brought together in the '20's Plenty!' concept which has a humanising effect on the street environment in urban areas. It does so by causing drivers to be travelling slowly enough, not only to recognise that other road-users have equal rights to be there, but also to be able to react in time to avoid accidents. For many years it has been understood that the 20 mph limit means that accidents, when they occur, are unlikely to be fatal, whereas there is a sharp increase in mortality as soon as speeds are higher.[11]

# KEY LESSONS

### THE ECONOMIC AND HEALTH BENEFITS OF DISCOURAGING PARKING

Limiting valuable urban space allocated to car parking frees it up for other uses, enabling the public realm to be more compact, stimulating, sociable, safe and economically successful. Private vehicle traffic using the streets to access parking causes air pollution including PM 2.5 and $CO_2$ emissions which between them contribute to respiratory illnesses and climate change. The combination of these factors makes a strong case for reducing urban centre car parking.

### BENEFIT FROM EXERCISE IN DAILY LIFE REDUCES THE LIKELIHOOD OF ILLNESSES CAUSED BY OBESITY

Choosing from the many options for active travel enables people to combine their daily business with getting the continual, low-level exercise that keeps them healthy. Increased adoption of active travel also generates the health benefits of social interaction.

### REDUCING HEALTH PROBLEMS CAUSED BY THE STRESS OF GETTING ABOUT

A more equitable approach to the use of urban space will lead to more efficient road systems and reduced levels of traffic congestion, making the experience of travel more agreeable and saving people time and money.

### FEWER CONCERNS ABOUT ROAD SAFETY AND RESPIRATORY ILLNESSES

The reduced dominance of motor vehicles in denser, urban environments leads to significant health improvements for all the other users of public space, with better air quality and less need to concentrate on avoiding traffic accidents.

### HOW TO REALISE THESE QUALITIES BY DESIGN?

- Provide dependable, interconnected, affordable public movement systems.
- Accept that electric vehicles are not ideal substitutes for fossil fuel vehicles as the PM 2.5 emissions caused by their brakes, tyres and road surfaces are all dangerous, toxic pollutants.

- Implement road space reallocation by making streets narrower, planting street trees and widening pavements to prioritise walking and reduce the impacts of pollutants caused by vehicle emissions on all users of the public realm.
- Treat emerging modes such as electric bikes and scooters as desirable and find the best ways to incorporate their use amongst other users of roads and areas of public realm.
- Demand that police enforce speed limits and local authorities monitor air quality to ensure they remain below health limits.
- Recognise that the thoughtful design of streets can be a more effective way to control traffic speeds than are speed limits.
- Adopt the '20's Plenty!' strategy to minimise accidents and reduce the risk of fatalities in those that do occur.
- Plan for gradual changes as street layouts become more equitable, and prepare a strategy for the transition period.
- Limit urban parking to reduce driving and encourage active travel.
- Discourage residential parking in urban centres or, if required, locate it below ground.
- To reduce the impacts of private cars in urban centres consider the options described, of 'carrot and stick', 'the nudge', 'from the top' and 'economic reality'.
- Monitor prospects for the introduction of CAVs and the disruption they may cause in the future.

# BERLINER PLATZ, ESSEN, GERMANY

*'The Perspektivenwerkstatt Essen Berliner Platz changed the city's policy on public participation and led to further highly successful placemaking projects in Essen, which otherwise could not have happened at all.'*

**HANS-JÜRGEN BEST**
Stadtdirektor (Chief Planner) of Essen.[12]

Berliner Platz, Essen, was a *Perspektivenwerkstatt* (community planning weekend) held by JTP and local partners in April 1999, focused on a 20 hectare brownfield site and adjacent redundant railway land that cut off the University of Essen from the town centre. The city's plans for completing the inner-city ring road would exacerbate the existing isolation of the university campus. This strategy was shelved.

## THE CHALLENGE

Controversy raged about the future of Essen's 'wild north', so called as it was a redundant tract of land occupied by the former heavy-industry site of the Krupp Works and adjacent unused railway land. Essen's cultural heart was to the south of the city centre, so traditionalists were opposed to the city's plan to construct a new concert hall on the isolated site to the north, leading to a plebiscite that stopped the initiative. The next idea was to have an open design competition. In Germany these are very well-organised but also expensive to run and do not necessarily produce desirable outcomes, particularly when the projects are complex and controversial. Recognising this predicament, Barbara Mettler -v. Meibom, Professor of Communications at the University of Essen, proposed that the funds earmarked for the competition be reallocated to a *Perspektivenwerkstatt* process which was duly approved by the city.

The site posed many dilemmas. The unfinished section of the inner ring road was in the city's '*B-Plan*' (framework plan) and programmed for completion, as the capacity of Friedrich-Ebert Strasse, the existing connection, was deemed inadequate. But the proposed route ran through the heart of the available site, thereby accentuating the isolation of Essen University that was already separated from the city centre by the redundant railway lines and hindered by an 'overall lack of north-south and east-west connections'. This was pointed out by landscape planner Hans Joachim Augustin and was relevant due to the city centre's acknowledged lack of evening activity and poor public safety record. These concerns could be ameliorated by better north-south connectivity that would increase footfall and activate the environment for much-needed inner city housing.

Applauded enthusiastically by the local community, the workshop vision represented in the simple diagram produced at the *Perspektivenwerkstatt*, Figure 3.4.5, reflected these ideas, showing the pedestrian/cycle route connecting the university with the city centre and crossing the central park which occupies the space where the ring road had been planned.

The 1999 *Perspektivenwerkstatt* results were adopted by politicians and local authorities as a consensus-based foundation for future projects and unlocked a major injection of funding for this important downtown area. Competing interests delayed realisation of the project for a further ten years, but since 2009 the area at Berliner Platz, now called *Universitätsviertel* (University Quarter) and also *Grüne Mitte Essen* (Green Centre Essen) is being delivered in several phases, still following the basic principles of the vision created through the original *Perspektivenwerkstatt* process.

**FIGURE 3.4.5**
CPW concept diagram –
connecting university with
town centre

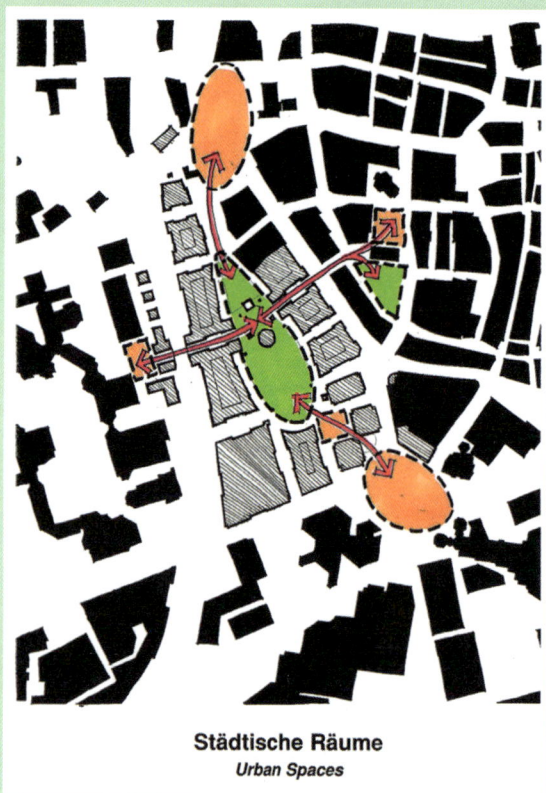

**Städtische Räume**
*Urban Spaces*

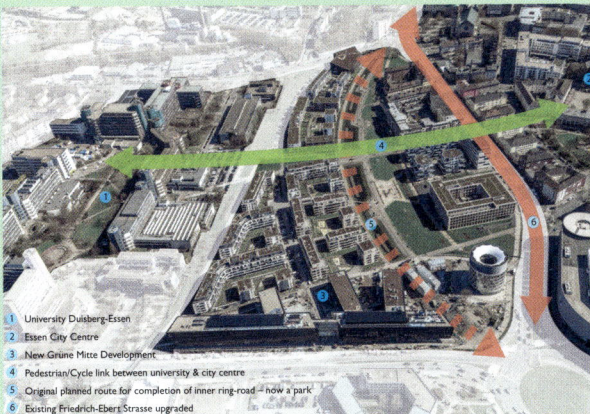

1 University Duisberg-Essen
2 Essen City Centre
3 New Grüne Mitte Development
4 Pedestrian/Cycle link between university & city centre
5 Original planned route for completion of inner ring-road – now a park
6 Existing Friedrich-Ebert Strasse upgraded

**FIGURE 3.4.6 A**
Grüne Mitte Essen annotated

**FIGURE 3.4.6 B**
Grüne Mitte Essen realised

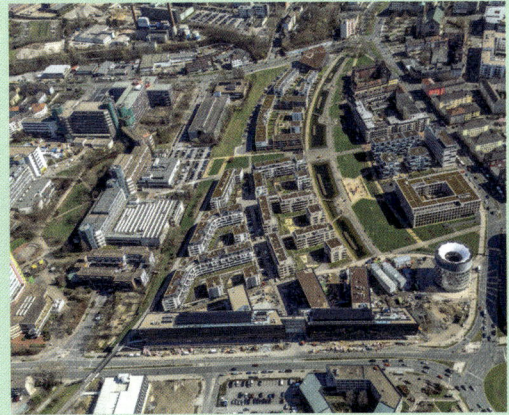

## THE OUTCOME

The *'B-Plan'* was amended to enable creation of a 2 hectare public park in the heart of the new neighbourhood that occupies the space previously allocated to the uncompleted ring road. This was a result of the city's newfound appetite for reducing vehicle traffic whereby the capacity of Friedrich-Ebert Strasse was deemed sufficient. The width of the railway corridor was reduced to allow for more mixed-use development on the now-enlarged site, including residential accommodation, and a new foot and cycle path provided a direct route through the *Universitätsviertel* from the university to the city centre, with a safe crossing over Friedrich-Ebert Strasse.

In terms of movement networks, the plan that has been realised is a good example of how transport systems can be adapted to a human scale, accommodating other uses and a wider range of priorities. It seems unlikely that the intended competition could have come up with such an outcome, not least because the planned ring road would have been a key element in the brief. So it is to the credit of the city planners that they agreed to open up the process to the local community, whose local knowledge and desire to live in a healthy environment emboldened the workshop team to produce a well-balanced and inherently flexible masterplan that could later be modified to create a new neighbourhood in the no longer 'wild north'.

# CASE STUDY 3.4.2
# OKLAHOMA CITY, USA

**FIGURE 3.4.7**
Introducing nature to breathe
life into streets

Mick Cornett, Mayor of Oklahoma City since 2004, had the vision to make major changes to the city's movement network as a means of addressing the city's problems of obesity. The success of these measures contributed to the raising of the city's profile and economic performance.

## THE PREDICAMENT

In 2004 the 600,000 population of the ultra-low density, car-dependent city with the nation's highest density of fast-food outlets, found itself ranked as the most obese in the USA. Facilities for pedestrians were very limited and little used but the highways were so wide there was no traffic congestion. One resident commented that 'you could get a speeding ticket during rush hour!' and in 2007 Mick Cornett's public announcement that 'this city is going on a diet and lose a million pounds!' started a conversation about the future.

**FIGURE 3.4.8** Places designed for walking

**FIGURE 3.4.9** The benefits of a generous sidewalk

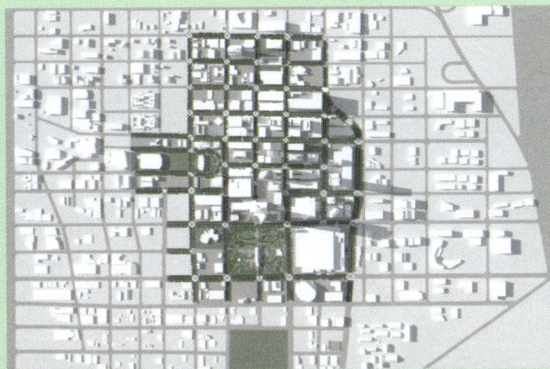

**FIGURE 3.4.10** Humanising the downtown grid

## CREATING A 'LABORATORY OF HEALTHY LIVING'

The city introduced a comprehensive programme of road space reallocation. The one-way traffic system was dismantled as it encouraged faster driving, inner-city highways were narrowed in favour of other modes of transport and sidewalks were widened and landscaped to be pedestrian-friendly. Hundreds of miles of new sidewalks were constructed to access schools and libraries, 100 miles of cycle routes were constructed and a downtown streetcar was introduced to increase walkability and support densification, 'designed around people, not cars'.

The 'million pounds' was lost in 2012 and the city was ranked the 22nd fittest in the USA. The introduction of additional health infrastructure included a new 78 acre central park and a world-class canoe, kayak and rowing centre. The cultural shift of prioritising health in this way attracted people in their 20s to move back to the city and the increased tax revenue this generated helped to finance the new facilities. Ian Birrell's article contains many examples of the reforms local people have made in response to Mick Cornett's inspirational leadership: 'There is no doubt Oklahoma City and its fat-fighting mayor deserve credit for their war against obesity, an inspiration for a country in which two-thirds of the population is overweight and has such a strong car culture.'[13]

# CHAPTER 3.5
# ENVIRONMENTAL INTEGRATION

**CASE STUDIES**
- Singapore
- London, UK

- Time spent in green spaces is good for our physical and mental health.
- Parks, play facilities, gardens and allotments are places that improve the quality of our lives and help to build community.
- Trees and shrubs contribute to comfortable microclimates and offer natural protection from flooding, strong winds and overheating.

*'Blue-green infrastructures are still not properly understood in their true function and value for the city and its inhabitants, as a background for liveability, and a dynamic repository resource to balance and stabilise life processes. That is the character of these flexible and ever-changing elements. One cannot measure, count and quantify the value of blue and green components in the urban structure as easily as one can the hard, built forms of engineered infrastructure, of buildings and real-estate developments.'*

**HERBERT DREISEITL**[1]

## INTRODUCTION

Major increases in the percentage of people living in cities are being projected across the planet. From a healthy placemaking perspective this can be a positive development as it suggests that urban structures will be compact, mixed-use environments at densities high enough for active travel to be the norm. In this 'city of short distances' there is potential for the public realm to be designed to high standards, encouraging more of us to enjoy the experiences on offer in lively social spaces.

The burgeoning value of property, and therefore of land, amongst the world's most successful cities incentivises developers to maximise floorplates and saleable space, creating buildings that soar ever higher. When these are for commercial uses it is assumed that over-shadowing and other environmental impacts are of lesser concern than they are for residential apartments. Given this appetite for urbanisation, there is a danger that the need for increased areas of green space to serve the growing urban population is not met. These are complex challenges to resolve both for residential areas and for places where commercial development prevails.

## THE IMPORTANCE OF GREEN SPACE FOR HEALTH

Vienna, Zürich and Singapore are cities that have produced coherent strategies for achieving a sustainable balance between green space and development. An essential aspect of this is to replace existing areas of low-density housing with taller blocks, thereby retaining the existing quantum of green space whilst increasing the number of people housed. The applicability of this approach depends on the housing policies and legislation regarding property ownership in different cities and countries.

Our positive response to green spaces is well-documented, amongst others by neuroscientific research originally carried out at universities in Denmark and Germany, that identified areas in the brain's cortex and amygdala that are triggered when we experience greenery. Stress is calmed, overall wellbeing increased and, since the 1980s, the medical profession has been in favour of incorporating greenery in the design of hospitals as it has been shown to benefit patients' recovery.

The 25% of the UK population that takes its dog for a walk gains health benefits from the exercise, fresh air and interaction with other dog-walkers. The need for a dog to have exercise is unquestioned, so if people would not otherwise go out then walking the dog is an important and valuable motivation to do so, with positive effects for the health of both parties.

**AT AN INDIVIDUAL LEVEL**

The importance of well looked-after urban space is set out by Kelsey Campbell-Dollaghan who celebrates the value of small urban interventions taking place in Philadelphia, based on work carried out in the University of Pennsylvania. She points out that the team's research 'paints a vivid picture of how our neighbourhoods impact our wellbeing and provides new evidence for why cities should be investing in low-cost but high-impact design interventions like lot greening in blighted neighbourhoods.'[2]

Dr Eugenia C South belongs to the team that studied the effects of these neglected green spaces and carried out a 'Psychological Distress Scale survey before and after the greenings, revealing a 40% reduction in feeling depressed and a 50% reduction in feeling worthless. The impact was even more pronounced in participants living below the poverty line'.[3]

Paris is the most densely populated city in the EU, with its public parks taking up only 9.5% of its area. Starting in 2015 the city agreed to grant a three-year *Permis de Végétaliser* (Permission to Plant) to citizens wishing to make the city greener.[4] The offer has been taken up by over 3,000 Parisiennes, creating small plots for greenery such as herbs, bee-friendly flowers and wall-climbing plants. The combination of local enthusiasm and support from City Hall has improved relationships, with the Mayor's Office recognising that it works better for the greening to be carried out by members of the community than by official administrators.

## TIME SPENT IN GREEN SPACES IS GOOD FOR OUR PHYSICAL AND MENTAL HEALTH

Access to greenery in all its forms can provide physical and mental solace from the claustrophobic pressures of contemporary life and the closer it is to where we live, work and learn, the more likely we are to use it.

Cities throughout mainland Europe have a tradition of small gardens and dachas in the countryside to which families 'retreat' at weekends. These compensate for the relative lack of private green space in cities, and the change of scene to more expansive environments is intrinsically therapeutic.

The compactness this allows in the cities is desirable in terms of healthy placemaking as it maximises convenience, encourages social interaction, supports the viability of retail and cultural facilities and makes the urban green spaces all the more valuable as readily-accessible places to relax.

The UK's tradition of houses with gardens contrasts with the urbanity of cities such as Paris and Moscow. Areas of private green space are available throughout the year and, for many people, gardening plays an important part in their lives.

Public parks in these residential areas offering accessible green space and sports facilities are important for apartment dwellers, and should be less than a 10-minute walk from home. But even with this criterion satisfied, without an equally short walk to retail and social facilities, this urban structure can give rise to extensive tracts of lower-density residential uses, generating longer travel distances and less viable public transport systems. This may lead to the drawbacks of urban sprawl, albeit to a lesser extent than that of the suburbs of many North American cities where car dependency is the norm. Atlanta, Oklahoma City, Vancouver and Toronto are some of the places that have been addressing these problems by densifying suburbia and providing facilities that encourage active travel.

## PARKS, PLAY FACILITIES, GARDENS AND ALLOTMENTS ARE PLACES THAT IMPROVE THE QUALITY OF OUR LIVES AND HELP TO BUILD COMMUNITY

For urban planners and landscape designers the range of options for green/blue spaces is very broad, with great scope to optimise the design opportunities presented by the context in which projects are located.

### DOMESTIC GARDENS AND ALLOTMENTS

Cities with substantial areas of terraced or detached houses will be low density and their private gardens contribute significant amounts of greenery. In addition to moderating variations in the climate, gardening is a generator of biodiversity due to the wide range of flowers, shrubs and trees chosen

**FIGURE 3.5.1**
The diversity of a domestic garden

at garden centres by the occupants. The birds and insects, especially bees, attracted by the greenery become valuable links in the food chain, often more resilient than non-urban green space, so much of which is exploited for industrial farming.

## GROWING

Allotments, orchards and small-holdings are sources of wellbeing for many reasons. In addition to the contribution they make to healthy diets, the growing of fresh produce or decorative flowers leads to physical and mental health benefits. These come from the natural and varied exercise involved in digging, planting and pruning, spending time outdoors breathing clean air and the mental satisfaction of nurturing growth and taking charge of a fundamental aspect of our lives.

Whether ornamental or edible, the experience of seeing plants grow is therapeutic both in maintaining mental health and as support for those

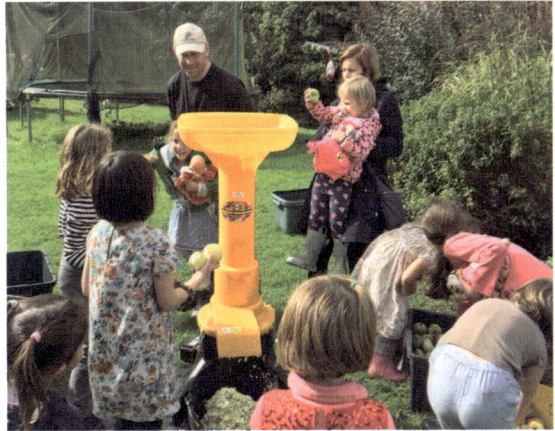

**FIGURE 3.5.2**
The health benefits of gardening – allotments in Yorkshire

**FIGURE 3.5.3**
Apple harvest and community interaction

trying to recover from mental illness. Allotment activity offers the benefit of creating a supportive community of allotment owners sharing the experience of communication whilst engaged in productive and energetic work.

The infectious enthusiasm of children can be seen in Figure 3.5.3 as they become involved with the process of turning fresh apples into juice.

## SUSTAINABLE DRAINAGE SYSTEMS (SUDS)

These include swales that make a virtue of necessity as conduits and 'sponges' for storm water attenuation. Usually linear in character, safe and well-overlooked, they can be designed as attractive walking routes that enliven residential environments with water-courses, greenery and the flora and fauna they bring with them.

## 'PLAY ON THE WAY'

Ideally these facilities can be incorporated into 'safe routes to school' and offer multiple benefits: awakening curiosity, getting exercise and breathing fresh air instead of traffic fumes. They can transform the chore of getting to school into something the children and parents/teachers look forward to. There is also evidence that conversations between parents and children when walking to and from school can be important and therapeutic. This may be because it is time spent between the clear 'bookends' of home and school; a specific purpose, with clear time limits. It offers scope for immediate reflection on the day at school that can involve so many types of social and physical stimuli, both positive and negative.

## WALKING BUS

The walking bus is another measure that contributes multiple benefits. Led by trusted adults, its 'safety in numbers' approach prioritises the physical health benefits of children getting to school on foot instead of in cars. But it also leads to their engagement with, and experience of, the 'real world' in a sociable atmosphere that differs from that of the classroom or playground. Where the footways run alongside vehicle-dominated routes, the aims of healthy placemaking will be best-served by wide pavements and the inclusion of street trees.

## LARGE PARKS

The intimacy of smaller green spaces within cities plays an essential role in softening the urban structure. The large spaces offer a much wider range of recreational facilities that include formal landscaping, informal space, water features, pitches for formal sports and interesting topography for more energetic walking. These can be complemented by a focus on the natural world, with sensory gardens, menageries, wild flower meadows and wetland habitats rich with biodiversity. They function as essential green lungs that are indispensable refuges for millions of city-dwellers.

## OPEN LANDSCAPE

Wilderness, national parks, Areas of Outstanding Natural Beauty (AONB) and stately homes and their grounds are typically in isolated locations, leaving no choice other than to access them by car. But, once there, footpath networks enable long walks often with characterful places to eat and drink on the way.

## LINEAR ROUTES

Often in urban settings, such as canals and former railway lines where facilities created as transport infrastructure have been abandoned and then re-purposed, these urban routes combine attractiveness and connectivity. The key strength shared by such places is that their original function was to link together different city neighbourhoods. Now they continue to do so, but as green foot and cycle routes instead of railway lines or working tow-paths, and these are all the more appreciated for the atmospheric, 19th-century infrastructure through which they pass.

Typically car-free yet easily accessed by large numbers of people, they are attractive not only for leisure and recreation but are also useful as direct shortcuts to other parts of town. Their special value with regard to health is that they combine the offer of a wide range of qualities with being linear. Although fundamentally active spaces, they can also incorporate places to stop and rest. This means that those using them can enjoy valuable exercise and relaxation in a stimulating, healthy environment.

The urban setting of Paris's elevated Promenade Plantée accommodates shops, businesses and galleries in the railway arches below and offers views onto the businesses and apartment buildings rising up on either side. Now a cherished Parisian attraction, it leads from the Bastille to the Bois de Vincennes and was the world's first elevated green walkway, created in 1993 by the adaptation of an abandoned mid-19th-century viaduct.

The High Line in New York City, a former railway line, is renowned for the way it enables people to cover large distances quickly, safely and in a beautifully designed, stimulating and sociable environment. Below are Manhattan's streets and avenues and its charm lies in the way the railway's geometry slaloms through the urban grid, offering unexpected vistas from elevated positions along the city's canyons, and giving rise to imaginatively-disposed buildings, many of which are recent structures that take advantage of their newfound visibility as seen from the route.

A particularly striking linear route is a boulevard running through the Lazienki Park in Warsaw. Poland's winters are cold and dark but, in the pitch-black woodland setting at 9 or 10 pm, a 2 km line of 5 m-high illuminated figures in elegant, courtly attire light up the route. Thousands of people including families with young children promenade along it; a magical

**FIGURE 3.5.4**
New York's High Line floating
above the busy streets

**FIGURE 3.5.5**
Evening promenade for the
whole family in Warsaw's
Lazienki Park

experience that combines the health benefits of an element of fantasy, contact with nature, sociability and exercise.

Places such as York, Chester, Carlisle and Dubrovnik have ancient city walls originally designed for defence in times of war and, when the threat of invasion had diminished, to control the movement of goods and people in and out of cities. The circular walks around these historic structures are now enjoyed by locals and tourists who can view the settlements from elevated vantage points and learn about the city's heritage from interpretation boards at the same time as getting exercise.

What is striking about all these linear routes is that, apart from a small number of die-hard joggers, the majority of users have not chosen to go there for exercise but because they are drawn to them as attractive and stimulating places in which to spend time. The invaluable exercise is a healthy bi-product of the interesting experience.

## TREES AND SHRUBS CONTRIBUTE TO COMFORTABLE MICROCLIMATES AND OFFER NATURAL PROTECTION FROM FLOODING, STRONG WINDS AND OVERHEATING

Green spaces and water bodies provide us with opportunities for leisure and recreation as well as moderating micro-climates by providing shade, absorbing pollutants and reducing wind speeds. Green space planted with trees contributes to the reduction of the urban heat island effect caused by concentrations of buildings and areas of hard landscaping. By lowering temperatures, the green space reduces energy consumption and the exhaust and emissions created by air-conditioning.

The bio-climatic effects of prevailing winds blowing over cool areas of landscape, such as water bodies, forests and parks, effectively provide free, natural air-conditioning for cities. The wind ventilates the urban environment because the convection currents caused by heat rising from buildings and paved areas suck in cool air from the green spaces and freshen the city's streets and squares.

As well as the role played by green spaces as respite from the hustle and bustle of urban life, greenery integrated into the streets themselves can have a transformative influence on people's daily habits. Sir Harry Burns, Professor of Global Health at the University of Strathclyde, has often cited the addition of street trees into a previously barren thoroughfare that can turn it into a place where people will choose to walk and linger.[5]

This increases the likelihood that they will interact with others attracted by the chance to spend time in a place where they feel comfortable. The social experience is complemented by the environmental and health benefits of urban greenery mentioned above.

Tree-lined streets also possess cachet, as reflected in street names such as 'Boulevard', 'Avenue', 'Gardens', 'Walk' and 'Park', even when the trees have been lost to the pressures of traffic or development – or perhaps were never there in the first place!

# KEY LESSONS

### MAXIMISE THE HEALTH BENEFITS OF TIME SPENT IN GREEN SPACE

Green space must be readily accessible from all dwellings and arranged to suit the varied needs of all members of the community.

### SEIZE OPPORTUNITIES TO CREATE OR EXTEND LINEAR ROUTES FOR PEDESTRIANS AND CYCLISTS

These can combine the benefits of significant amounts of exercise on interesting paths with breathing clean air, experiencing biodiversity, the potential for social interaction and accessing destinations in other parts of town. Doing so avoids the need to cross roads, risk vehicle accidents, inhale polluted air or be disturbed by noisy traffic, including emergency vehicles.

### MAKE THE MOST OF THE NATURAL BENEFITS OF GREEN SPACE

Incorporate green spaces as the natural and sustainable way to moderate extremes of climate. Combine the practical measures with imaginative landscape designs that raise the spirits, helping to provide wellbeing; mental as well as physical.

### HOW TO REALISE THESE QUALITIES BY DESIGN?

- Use linear routes to combine exercise with going to destinations including 'play on the way' and the 'walking bus'.
- Link green spaces together to maximise the benefits of 'green corridors', for people as well as wildlife.
- Create nature trails, areas of wetland and coastal walks as destinations where people of all ages can learn more about nature and the support it needs to survive the habitat loss created by humans that is devastating the natural world on which we also depend.
- Promote the benefits of gardens and gardening; exercise, fresh air and being in control, and of allotments; fresh food, watching plants grow and social interaction.

- Ensure that accessible and safe green space is no more than 10-minutes' walk from all dwellings.
- Introduce small urban greenspace interventions that make a big difference.
- Design areas of green/blue technical infrastructure, such as stormwater attenuation, so they are safe and can serve as high quality, public amenity spaces.
- Incorporate green space wherever possible, including for vertical greening and on balconies and green roof terraces. As well as providing amenity space for residents, this helps to attenuate storm water runoff.
- Plant trees to slow wind speeds and absorb pollutants and reduce urban heat island effects with natural cooling that reduces the need for air-conditioning.
- Ensure densification projects allow for more public green space, not less, and that developments cause no unacceptable overshadowing of neighbouring buildings or green spaces.
- Harness the benefits of bio-climatic design by using nature to create comfortable micro-climates.

# CASE STUDY 3.5.1
# SINGAPORE

**FIGURE 3.5.6**
Bishan Park watercourse and landscaped mound with artwork

Singapore became independent in 1965, having been a city of slums, congestion, open sewers and unemployment. Despite lacking natural resources, in 50 years it has been transformed into a clean, modern metropolis with a diversified economy and reliable infrastructure.

The city has applied ingenuity and imagination in combining areas of very high-density buildings with extensive tracts of green and blue space. By 2030, the city's plan is for at least 85% of residents to be living within a 10-minute walk of a park. An incentive programme was introduced to replace green space lost at ground level due to new development with high-level greenery on terraces and gardens that provide new opportunities for social interaction.

Innovative design reduces the feeling of density by the use of 'green' and 'blue' elements. Parks, rivers, and ponds are interspersed with high-rise buildings, and the bodies of water also double as flood-control mechanisms.

Some 3 million trees have been planted in Singapore, including a stand of virgin rainforest, rich in biodiversity, in the heart of the island.[6]

## BISHAN PARK

This park was created through the transformation of an existing, single-use drainage channel into a much-loved public open space. The old concrete channel was dead-straight, having been designed to discharge water into the sea as quickly as possible. The new concept slows the flow of water by creating a natural river bed, with soft-landscaping that stabilises the banks and reduces erosion. The width of the meandering course varies along its length, combining the attenuation of stormwater with its qualities as an attractive landscape feature enjoyed by visitors and residents of the adjacent apartment blocks that overlook the park.

The redundant concrete was recycled as substrate for the new river bed and piled up to create landscaped mounds for public art installations.

**FIGURE 3.5.7**
Bishan Park river panorama, before – an inaccessible concrete drain

**FIGURE 3.5.8**
Bishan Park river panorama, after – a sustainable green space that prevents flooding

The success of the project, which also addresses the need for clean water for domestic use, means there is now increased demand in Singapore for projects of this kind.

A number of projects highlight Singapore's determination to lead the way in environmental integration in high density urban environments. Many such structures in Singapore are tourist attractions, luxury hotels and care facilities that demonstrate the possibilities for integrating greenery and nature in tall buildings.

## KHOO TECK PUAT HOSPITAL

This Biophilic Hospital is both a hospital in a garden and a garden in a hospital. The 102,000 m², 590-bed public facility integrates large amounts of greenery in its architecture and offers a healing environment by appealing to the senses of sight, smell and sound. These are provided by abundant greenery and water features, the aroma of plants and the sound of falling water. The hospital won the Stephen R Kellert Biophilic Design Award as it embraces the belief that humans feel healthier in environments connected to their natural surroundings.[7]

**FIGURE 3.5.9**
Kampung Admiralty Centre – the health benefits of greenery

**FIGURE 3.5.10**
Northpoint City, Yishun –
mixed-uses and apartments
with prolific greenery

## KAMPUNG ADMIRALTY CENTRE

WOHA architects designed a healthy, green building at the Kampung Admiralty Centre, where senior citizens can live in maximum comfort. The scheme consists of three layers; an internal Community Plaza at the lower levels, a Medical Centre in the middle and an elevated Community Park at the top, with apartments for seniors. By integrating healthcare, social and commercial amenities in one structure, the building's design helps to bridge age differences and encourage active ageing.

## NORTHPOINT CITY

This area, designed by SAA Group Architects is a major mixed-use development in northern Singapore incorporating social and recreation facilities, a rooftop community garden, 920 apartments and a below-ground transport hub.

Two up-market hotels designed by WOHA Architects, Parkroyal and OASIA, take every opportunity to show how greenery can be introduced in dense cities.

**FIGURE 3.5.11** Parkroyal cascading plants

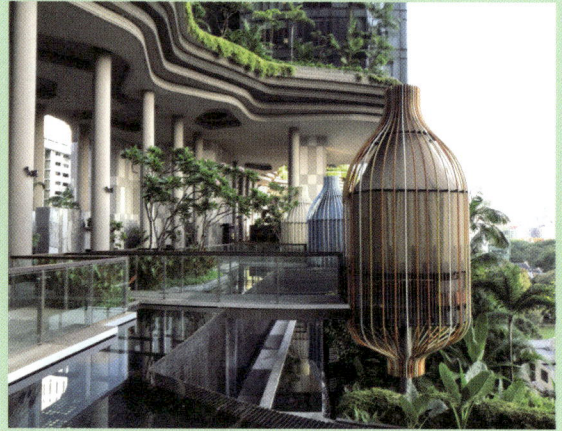

**FIGURE 3.5.12** Parkroyal integrated water features

**FIGURE 3.5.13** Oasia Hotel , a 'green tour-de-force'

## PARKROYAL HOTEL

Vertical gardens at the 5 star Parkroyal Hotel help save costs for building owners by cooling surface temperatures and reducing the need for air-conditioning. Plant-covered balconies and terraces around the exterior provide 15,000 m² of greenery, close to twice that of the site area, and an elevated pool provides a further environmental attraction.[8]

## OASIA HOTEL

The Oasia Hotel 'Living Tower' is a green tour-de-force that deploys a wide variety of techniques to redistribute urban greenery on the vertical plane.[9]

# CASE STUDY 3.5.2
# LONDON, UK

**FIGURE 3.5.14**
Workers' lunchbreak in
St John's Cloister, Clerkenwell

Estimates of the percentage of green space in cities around the world vary according to where boundaries have been drawn and how land use areas have been calculated. Calculations of the percentage of green space in London are also widely divergent, being dependent on the inclusion or exclusion of domestic gardens and of any paved areas within those gardens.[10]

Compared with other world cities, London is low-density, with large areas of housing of four storeys or fewer and generous quantities of green space. The city has an admirable variety of green spaces, a major attraction for residents and visitors alike; from pocket parks to linear greenways and major open spaces.

## POCKET PARKS AND CHURCHYARDS

Often hidden in unexpected places within the dense urban 'jungle', these atmospheric places provide an excuse to get away from the work station, relax in peace and quiet or convene in an outdoor lunch spot to enjoy the open air with friends and colleagues.

## URBAN SQUARES

Iconic 'London Squares' such as Russell Square and Tavistock Square in Bloomsbury and Lincoln's Inn Fields in Holborn are effective foils for the high quality buildings that frame them. They are greatly admired for the contribution they make to the townscape as well as being a valuable amenity for locals and visitors. Not all London squares are open to the public but even the private ones contribute greenery, elegance and bio-climatic cooling to the urban fabric. The recently-created Granary Square is the focal space of Argent's King's Cross development, accessible from every side and surrounded by a rich variety of cultural and leisure uses. Although clearly structured by regenerated industrial buildings, it has an informal layout with a playful fountain grid as a centrepiece that is strong magnet at all times of year, but especially during heatwaves.

**FIGURE 3.5.15**
During a heatwave in Granary Square, King's Cross

**FIGURE 3.5.16**
Hampstead Heath –
a spacious, soothing resource,
full of variety

## LARGE SCALE PARKS

The biggest London parks, such as Richmond Park, Wimbledon Common, Hampstead Heath, Hyde Park, Regent's Park, Victoria Park, Bushy Park, Clapham Common, Battersea Park, Greenwich Park and Queen Elizabeth Olympic Park, are dotted around the city. Perhaps these hark back to the village structure on which the modern metropolis is founded, each with its own distinct character. Those on higher ground outside the city centre, such as Greenwich Park, location of the Royal Observatory and the Prime Meridian Line, and Hampstead Heath, offer sweeping views over the city. In others, such as Hyde Park and Regent's Park, with minimal topographical variation, it is large water-bodies that act as key attractions, including the lake for model boats.

## LINEAR PARKS

**Parkland Walk Local Nature Reserve, London Borough of Haringey**

This four and a half mile long abandoned railway line, which runs past the rear gardens of dwellings connecting Finsbury Park and Alexandra Palace, has steep embankments on either side. Providing a direct link from Finsbury Park to Highgate and beyond, the informal landscape design fulfils multiple functions. The route's relaxed, almost rural, feel offers a biodiversity-rich green corridor, pleasant walks, cycle rides and places for outward-bound initiatives such as adventure playgrounds and rock-climbing walls. Regular footfall and proximity to the houses glimpsed through foliage mean that it feels safe to spend time there, and the practical advantage of a direct, healthy, car-free route to these different parts of the city is an asset appreciated by large numbers of people.

**FIGURE 3.5.17** Regent's Canal – London's 'Low Line' 1 – a beautiful place to walk

**FIGURE 3.5.18** Regent's Canal – London's 'Low Line' 2 – retention of industrial heritage

## Regent's Canal, London Borough of Camden

This waterside route could well be referred to as London's 'Low Line'. The canal walk's sunken level endows it with a sense of discovery enhanced both by the presence of water and by colourful, idiosyncratic barges, now re-purposed for leisure trips or as dwellings, that offer historical continuity with the canal's original purpose. People are attracted by it as a route and by the free entertainment on offer. This includes glimpses of exotic animals and birds where the canal runs below and through London Zoo, and the mechanical engineering dramas, guaranteed to draw crowds fascinated by watching the lock-gates being operated, using the same technology as in days gone by. The limited headroom under some of the canal bridges adds an agreeable authenticity to the experience.

## Thames Path and South Bank

The Thames Path runs for 184 miles from the river's source near Cirencester in Gloucestershire to the Thames Barrier in Greenwich. Although it follows the river bank as much as possible there are interruptions due to private land ownership. Where possible these are being acquired bit by bit to maintain continuity. The path runs through the cultural magnet of the South Bank with its concert halls, theatres, galleries, museums and food and drink outlets, its highest intensity extending 3.5 km from the London Eye in the west to Shad Thames in the east.

# CHAPTER 3.6
# COMMUNITY EMPOWERMENT

- Communities become emotionally attached to the design of their neighbourhoods, enhancing their quality of life.
- The sense of collaboration is a potent force that strengthens social networks, raises aspirations and leads to positive change.

*'Nimbies get created by top-down decision-makers!'*

**JIM DIERS**[1]

## INTRODUCTION

The spatial considerations relating to community empowerment are interwoven with the motivation of the local inhabitants to shape their environments.

The involvement of communities is activated when they see the potential for their immediate environments to be enhanced. Strong opinions, based on understanding and experience of how the place could and should work, strengthen their determination to make it happen. That combination of knowledge and determination can give rise to energetic, collective creativity that makes high quality outcomes likely. These may become a source of civic pride, not only because of the quality of what has been achieved but also as a result of the part local people have played in the process.

The dynamics of community empowerment are influenced by the different personalities who have a stake in a given area. Amongst them will be those with the sense of leadership and skills to fulfil a mission shared by the community, supported by others committed to the process and keen to contribute to its realisation.

The concept of community is not simple. Typical definitions refer to it as 'a group of people with a common characteristic or interest living together within a larger society'.[2]

Most people have a sense of what 'community' means and could relate their personal interpretation of it to the above definition. But, when applied to human settlements, it is important to appreciate that the communality also needs to accommodate differing opinions and diversity, as these are key aspects of what makes a community tick. The expression 'within a larger society' is cogent, as communities vary in size and their memberships and boundaries are by no means fixed.

Wanting to feel part of an inclusive and equitable community is an aspect of human nature. It involves balancing the diverse needs of individuals and groups through well-managed processes to which they can contribute.

## COMMUNITIES BECOME EMOTIONALLY ATTACHED TO THE DESIGN OF THEIR NEIGHBOURHOODS, ENHANCING THEIR QUALITY OF LIFE

To fulfil the principles of healthy placemaking a neighbourhood needs to be a place where people feel comfortable and safe. That requires streets to be well-overlooked and animated by people walking and cycling, pavements to be shaded by street trees, and a dependable public transport network to keep things running smoothly.

Combine these qualities with human-scale spaces and a local centre nearby and the ingredients are in place for a community to thrive. However, these conditions do not just materialise of their own accord, but arise out of long-term, strategic decision-making that has proved its value over time and become accepted and established. So long as this virtuous circle of good-governance continues, the need to protest may be low. However, the wish to contribute is likely to be maintained by the community's desire to make their home even more of a success and to enhance its reputation further. Civic pride is a force to be reckoned with.

Communities become activated when the opposite scenario prevails, when the locals see that the places where they lead their lives are suffering because the way it is governed is unsatisfactory. This is when they believe they have no choice but to take matters into their own hands and conclude that positive action is a necessity. They may decide to handle the situation internally or seek support from outside agencies. The local authority is usually a helpful ally but is sometimes part of the problem, in which case the challenge is all the greater.

A community that has developed in the fertile soil of a healthy urban infrastructure also needs well-designed public buildings and external spaces in which to hold meetings and events when going about its business. That business is the central theme for this section.

Settlements managed well enough to be thriving will have earned trust and respect. This does not mean everyone agrees with every decision but, provided there is a system of communication leading to outcomes that are seen to be fair, the virtuous circle can be maintained. Sustaining the circle is difficult within a political system consisting of competing interest groups pursuing differing agendas. High level political considerations frequently override issues that local activists know to be essential to the continuation of the community's support mechanisms. This is the point when community voices need to be heard.

## INEQUALITY

Inequality is one of the most divisive aspects of the increasingly materialistic environments in which so many people live. The huge differentials between the wealth of countries around the world mean that those with fewer resources face challenges different from those that are the primary focus of this book. The citizens of less well-off countries continue to suffer from sicknesses that are cured routinely elsewhere and are afflicted by causes of mortality long since eradicated in more affluent nations.

But huge differentials also prevail within those affluent countries. Experiencing this can lead to a disempowering sense of detachment from the unattainable lifestyles of the more fortunate sectors of society. In most countries, support is provided through initiatives set up by governments, local authorities, religious organisations, charities and philanthropic groups aiming to overcome inequality and lack of opportunity.

There are also 'bottom-up' approaches, such as asset-based community development (ABCD) introduced to help disadvantaged citizens find ways out of their unsatisfactory circumstances and gain in confidence and self-esteem. It starts from the assumption that everyone and every place has underutilised strengths and resources that can be mobilised for mutual support and community initiatives. One of its guiding principles, of particular relevance to healthy placemaking, addresses the psychological effects of being disempowered through the creation of a culture of dependency: 'The Welfare system today works in such a way that professionals have made clients and recipients of the poor, robbing them of the support from their neighbours who now think that they are not skilled enough to help. This leads to isolation of the individuals. The poor begin to see themselves as people with special needs that can only be met by outsiders, but this can be changed through the ABCD process.'[3]

Communities are diverse and potent networks of gifts and assets, each with a unique set of capabilities to channel the potential of local people towards the improvement of their communities. ABCD's approach summarises assets into five categories whose collective impacts can unlock opportunities for positive change:

1. Individuals are at the centre of ABCD, as everyone has valuable assets and gifts.
2. Associations are informal groups, such as clubs, that congregate around common interests without seeking to have control over them.
3. Institutions are paid groups of people, typically professional organisations, whose assets help the community to capture valuable resources and establish a sense of responsibility for urban initiatives.
4. Physical assets include property in the form of land, buildings, space or funds that can be used to enable projects to be realised.
5. Connections bring people together, sharing their assets by bartering and exchanging, typically done through the building of relationships between individuals.

'Time banking' is one of many tools that ABCD can mobilise to tap local assets by placing a value on citizens' personal resources and abilities. Time banking involves individuals or organisations exchanging their time, instead of money, by providing skills for one another. Each person's hour has the same value, regardless of the financial value that the services would have in normal business transactions, and this reciprocity has shown itself to build the confidence, trust and respect that help to forge relationships and strengthen community cohesion.[4]

With increasing longevity worldwide there are many in retirement who still have much to offer but lack a business model that works for the level of activity which suits them, or the financial resources to pay for help. Whether it is gardening, car or house repairs, administrative tasks, music lessons or language translation or classes, the process can broaden horizons and widen circles of acquaintance. The approach is promoted by the medical profession due to the psychological effects it can have as a positive form of therapy, free of stigmatisation.

These examples serve as reminders of how our resourcefulness and resilience can be activated by creating the right conditions, and the many benefits that are opened up when people's spirits are raised and they feel included and empowered rather than marginalised.

## THE SENSE OF COLLABORATION IS A POTENT FORCE THAT STRENGTHENS SOCIAL NETWORKS, RAISES ASPIRATIONS AND LEADS TO POSITIVE CHANGE

### PARTICIPATORY PLANNING – COMMUNITY PLANNING PROCESS

#### METHODOLOGY
Practitioners use different methodologies for collaborative planning processes, and a tried and tested approach is set out in RIBA Publishing's book *20/20 Visions* in which the author Charles Campion focuses on collaborative planning and placemaking. His comment that 'through shared working from an early stage, communities and businesses can help shape and support development

that is right for their specific place, and will enable it to grow and thrive' goes to the heart of why community planning is of such importance.[5]

The first step is to make sure that the project and its location are suited to be the focus of a community planning process. In all scenarios there will be a preparatory phase, normally of four to eight weeks, involving research and analysis regarding the project's physical, social, economic and environmental context. Publicity for the event in local newspapers, on the radio, the internet, social media and mail-drops starts a month or so in advance to give the local community sufficient notice that a public process is to take place, reinforced a few weeks later by a public launch.

As community planning is a concept new to most people, a further element at this stage is 'Community Animation' where team members visit the locality and engage in planned or informal, face to face conversations with local residents and stakeholders. This has two key aspects: to clarify what is to take place at the public event and for the team to learn about issues of local or wider concern not previously identified by the research carried out to date.

These networks enable collaboration and the sharing of knowledge, as was the case in a project in Arnsberg, North-Rhine-Westphalia, Germany. The local authority's steering group decided to expand its range by forming a support circle of local people. Each attendee was to contribute by providing advance information about the project to their network of contacts to generate widespread attendance by well-informed, local people at the event itself.

A special bonus arose regarding the project's publicity during the build-up to the participatory event. During an early support circle meeting, the owner of a printing company volunteered to print the project programme on the paper bags in which local bakeries sell their loaves, so the message would be accessible to everyone in Arnsberg who bought bread. This demonstrated the cohesiveness of the community in precisely the way the steering group had hoped and sent out a message of inclusivity that bore fruit deep within the local culture.

The primary focus of the process is the public engagement stage known as a 'Charrette'; a brainstorming exercise that lasts anything from a few days to a week, depending on the project's size and scope. As explained in the document, 'Collaborative Planning for All': 'A Charrette is a collaborative event that engages local people with expert facilitation in co-creating spatial plans and designs for their place. It is a hands-on approach with stated goals that allows for feedback and design changes, important for gaining stakeholder understanding and support.'[6]

The Charrette consists of public workshops on key topics facilitated by a multi-disciplinary team using two basic formats – 'post-it workshops' and 'hands-on-planning tables'. In the post-it workshop the participants write comments on the yellow notes and hand them to the facilitators who read them out, air points requiring clarification and categorise the ideas by arranging them on sheets of flip-chart paper on the wall. This methodology is rapid, thorough, transparent and more engaging than the public meetings to which people are accustomed.

The second format is 'hands-on-planning' for which a number of smaller groups facilitated by urban planners gather around tables to work on the further development of the ideas that had emerged during the post-it workshops. Each group explores ideas on base plans and generate concepts that are presented immediately at plenary sessions for all to consider. Rather than being explained by facilitators, to empower the participants the ideas are reported back by workshop members, including school children.

The combined outcomes of the two types of workshop provide invaluable information to guide the design team members who work continuously for several days to produce a 'Report Back' presentation. This consists of a set of 'Key Themes' summarising the most important strategic, social and economic issues, and a physical 'Vison Plan' that integrates the strongest design concepts that had emerged. Diagrams, cartoons and verbatim quotes are incorporated in an illustrated broadsheet that summarises the overall Charrette process and is distributed at the end of the Report Back presentation.

The Charrette is a key component in Community Planning, establishing a natural platform for sharing knowledge and gaining new insights. High intensity brainstorming methods deliver consensus points very quickly that flow into broad concepts to be adapted and refined as fresh information and ideas

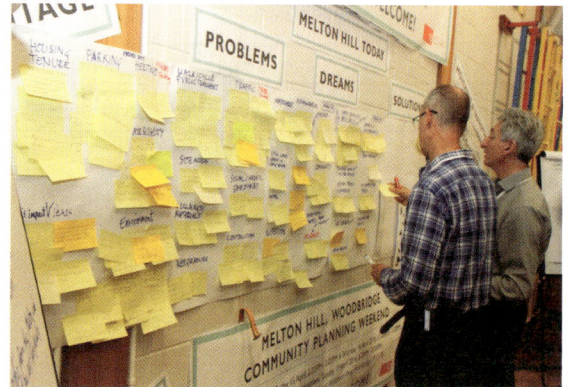

emerge. Joel Mills, Director of 'Communities By Design' and a key figure of the American Institute of Architects (AIA) summarises the value of this way of collaborative working as follows: 'The grassroots Charrette process provides the democratic vehicle for citizens to participate actively in designing and creating places that represent the collective contributions of all. Through the Charrette process, we are empowering people to revitalise our cities and our democratic values from the bottom up.'[7]

The version outlined above is based on a 'Community Planning Weekend', typically beginning on a Thursday or Friday, continuing over the weekend and with the 'Report Back' on a Tuesday or Wednesday. This Charrette process that progresses in a few days from first thoughts to an integrated, consensus vision is valued for its immediacy and makes a strong impression, helping participants and team members to retain their grasp on the overall ideas that have been generated. This concentrated timescale contrasts with traditional urban planning processes that may take weeks and months to arrive at initial concepts.

Participants witness how their collective input combined with the expertise of the professional team produces a vision that incorporates and integrates the most important issues, and the speed of the process is greatly welcomed. The Vision Plan is a high-level, broad-brush drawing, but what it lacks in detailed design is in most cases more than compensated for by the 'buy-in' of the local community, the design team and the client.

Clarity, openness and sensitive handling of the workshops by the facilitators build trust amongst the participants, and tipping points often occur when the opinions of local individuals or groups are expressed, and it becomes evident that there are other members of the community with views that differ from their own. This can introduce a more balanced, and indeed healthier, equilibrium between the facilitators and the differing priorities of the participants.

The community empowerment that is opened up by the participatory planning process is typically a positive experience that is refreshingly new to most of those who attend. The combination of social interaction and the broadening of horizons as a result of gaining a better understanding is itself a healthy 'learning-journey'. The fundamental logic of the collaborative process

**FIGURE 3.6.3**
Community planning event invitation

**Help shape the vision for the future of our cattle market**

Have your say...

Friday 8 March to Tuesday 12 March 2019

EVERYONE WELCOME

**Public Sessions**

Background exhibition and community workshops
Venue: The Liskerrett Community Centre, Varley Lane, Liskeard PL14 4AP
Friday 8 March 1.45pm - 5.30pm
Saturday 9 March 11.00am - 4.00pm

**Report back presentation**
Eliot House Hotel, Castle Street, Liskeard PL14 3AU
Tuesday 12 March 6.30pm - 8.00pm

CORNWALL COUNCIL
LISKEARD COUNCIL
jtp
Ministry of Housing, Communities & Local Government

**Report back presentation**

**Tuesday 12 March 2019**
Eliot House Hotel, Castle Street, Liskeard PL14 3AU
6.30pm   Doors open
6.45pm   Report back of the vision for Liskeard cattle market
8.00pm   Close

EVERYONE WELCOME

**Liskeard Cattle Market Charrette**

Friday 8 March to Tuesday 12 March 2019

You are invited to the Liskeard Cattle Market Charrette (Community Planning Weekend) to help shape the Vision for the future of this important site and its relationship with the town.

The Liskeard Cattle Market Charrette is part of the Ministry of Housing, Communities and Local Government (MHCLG) exemplar charrette programme, designed to promote innovative and effective community engagement, to achieve design quality. For more information please visit **jtp.co.uk/projects/liskeard** or contact the JTP Community Planning team at **community@jtp.co.uk** or on Freephone **0800 0126730**.

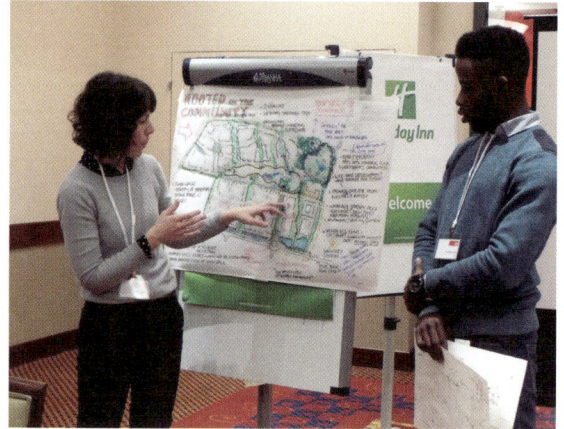

**FIGURE 3.6.4**
Community planning
weekend – hands-on-planning
tables in action

**FIGURE 3.6.5**
Landscape workshop
– hands-on-planning
feedback

is to learn at the outset of the project not only about likely points of contention but also all the positive aspirations the community may have. This allows concerns to be addressed and hopes to be incorporated in the design as it evolves, often including focus groups convening after the event to address specific topics.

## LANDSCAPE WORKSHOPS

In the design of masterplans, landscape workshops held at an early stage in a project's development have proved to be an exciting and enjoyable way to involve local communities in the design process. The aim is to establish principles for the green/blue infrastructure and comes with the tacit understanding that these can only be delivered by a development that will fund them, but also helps local people to recognise that development can have positive outcomes.

# KEY LESSONS

### COMMUNITY INVOLVEMENT WITH PARTICIPATORY INITIATIVES

Collaborating with people with an appetite for community activism and campaigning on local issues is a rewarding experience that can produce positive outcomes and lead to increased cohesion amongst citizens. Enjoyable public events can reinforce civic pride and celebrate the contributions of local people.

### ADDRESSING INEQUALITY AND SOCIAL EXCLUSION

Strengthen community cohesion by encouraging people in need of help to sign up for 'bottom-up' support schemes such as asset-based community development (ABCD) and time-banking. These can empower participants to gain in confidence, make new contacts and help one another by reciprocating on the skills they can offer.

### REDUCING THE EFFECTS OF LONELINESS AND ISOLATION

Meeting other people in a supportive context and encouraging social diversity and inclusiveness can increase people's confidence enough to engage in social interaction. Productive, shared activities such as gardening and adult education programmes generate new experiences and expand horizons.

### HOW TO REALISE THESE QUALITIES BY DESIGN?

- Enable people to feel comfortable and safe, create well-overlooked, animated, well-maintained streets lined, where possible, with trees.
- Enable community activities by providing well-equipped facilities where groups can hold meetings, attend events and make contact with other interest-groups. These should be attractive, accessible environments that make social interaction easy.
- Promote participatory events to empower local people to contribute their design ideas and knowledge of their area to planning projects. This will assist their learning about the projects' background and forge new allegiances with other members of the community.

- Do not underestimate the wisdom people have about the places where they live, and the importance of respecting feelings of civic pride.
- Provide support to groups motivated to shape their environments and take matters into their own hands when there is no alternative.
- Find ways to minimise social inequality and build confidence, including inputs from community support organisations and bottom-up strategies such as ABCD and time banking.
- Recognise participatory planning Charrettes as learning processes for everyone and the chance for participants to share new ideas. They are also an opportunity for the attendees to find out about innovative approaches developed elsewhere that could provide inspiration for the future of the place where they live.
- Organise landscape workshops to emphasise the benefits development can offer to concerned, neighbouring communities. An example could be previously inaccessible areas of green space being opened to the public as a result of new development.
- Accept that differences of opinion in communities are healthy provided the aim is how best to serve the whole community and is not manipulated by self-interest groups intent on marginalising others.

# CAPITOL HILL, SEATTLE, USA

## THE BACKGROUND

Capitol Hill is a neighbourhood located towards the southern end of Seattle's East District. It provides an excellent example of how a community's convictions and determination were able to influence the processes by which the neighbourhood responded to change. This is graphically chronicled in a paper written in 2006 by Kay Rood in describing her volunteer leadership over ten years with the community organisation 'Groundswell Off Broadway'.[8] The highs and lows she experienced reflected the realities of working together to empower communities.

## THE PROCESS

A park, originally designed in the early 20th century by the Olmstead Brothers, renowned American landscape architects, had become increasingly run-down and was shunned by the local community. Local activists began the process of its regeneration in 1993, culminating in a triumphant re-opening in September 2005. As stated by Kay Rood, who volunteered with the community organisation, 'Groundswell Off Broadway' for over ten years: 'The long-awaited rejuvenation brought renewal not only to our neighbourhood park but to the whole community ... an historic place, connecting our neighbourhood to not only city, but national, history'. Initially called Lincoln Park, it was renamed Cal Anderson Park as a tribute to the State Senator who had worked tirelessly on behalf of the disenfranchised and died of AIDS in August 1995, just as Groundswell was mobilising on this first big-grant project. By taking the initiative in choosing that name the community was signalling that the neighbourhood's identity was gaining strength.

As the project got underway, Groundswell leafleted the wider community asking the question: 'What Do You Want for Your Park'? This involved working with the planning authorities whose attitude, Rood realised, seemed to veer back and forth between support and resistance. She learned that

**FIGURE 3.6.6**
Cal Anderson Park – peaceful

**FIGURE 3.6.7**
Cal Anderson Park – protest

positive approaches tended to lead to positive outcomes, but that good ideas proposed by the public were likely to be dismissed. To address this contradiction, she commented that 'We always strove to get the City to realise that our goals and their goals were essentially the same.'

With her growing experience as a negotiator driving the project forward, the on-site work began in earnest in 2001 when the existing restroom was demolished: 'That restroom was the symbol of everything that was wrong with the old park – unsafe, unsightly, inaccessible. I never knew slinging a sledge hammer could be so satisfying!' This helped Rood to understand how important her de facto job had become, because the community's expectations were now at such a high level. That fact that Groundswell's existence had generated an active community group campaigning for the park gave them a significant status in the decision-making process.

Looking back at the whole experience, three of Rood's comments summarise her experience: 'This was a once-in-a-lifetime chance to build a truly world-class urban park … I mostly felt lucky to be part of an effort that resulted in creating a place with such a lasting legacy … The biggest gratification is that the variety of uses is as wide as the variety of people.'[9]

**FIGURE 3.6.8**
Tribute gathering – an
emotional celebration

## THE FOLLOW-UP

Cal Anderson Park is in the Pine Street and
Broadway area and is the most iconic community
landmark in the southern part of the wider
Capitol Hill neighbourhood. A series of other
community initiatives add to its significance,
many of them centred around Broadway
Crossing on Pine Street.

The grocery chain store Walgreens was
planning one of its standard, single-storey
buildings, set back behind a forecourt of parking
spaces, on the south-west corner of Broadway
Crossing. The plans had become sufficiently
contentious to reach version no. 6, due to constant
resistance from the local community, although
the developers still expected to have their way in
the end. But the locals, supported by the Capitol
Hill Housing Group, were insistent that Walgreens'
proposals represented a poor use of space and a
missed opportunity, as the corner needed proper
spatial definition. Walgreens finally conceded to
the stubborn persistence of this empowered community, agreeing to build a
mixed-use store with four floors of affordable housing above, their first ever in
the whole of the USA.

In the main entrance to a community space in the completed building
at Broadway Crossing, citizens attended the inauguration of a plaque with
a dedication to Ann Donovan: 'The power of community is real. If not for
the actions of a few members of the Capitol Hill community in 2003, you
would be standing in a car park right now. Their action, through the Capitol
Hill Community Council and under leadership of Ann Donovan, led to a far
better solution: a multi-use building with affordable homes for families in
the heart of our walkable, vibrant neighbourhood.' This committed group
of local people had managed to overcome the might of a corporate

**FIGURE 3.6.9** Jimi Hendrix Statue – celebrating a local hero

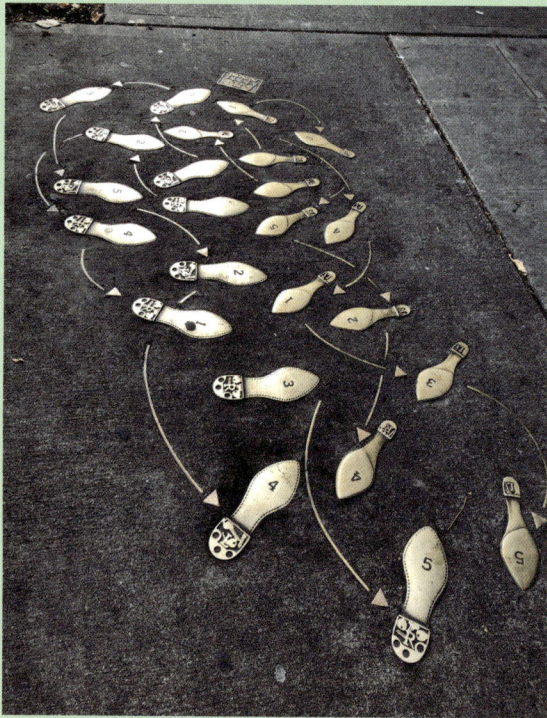

**FIGURE 3.6.10** Cha-cha-cha dance steps on a sidewalk

organisation, applying their knowledge and sense of social justice to arrive at an outcome that delivered multiple benefits for the Capitol Hill neighbourhood.

## CELEBRATING AND HONOURING IDENTITY

Jimi Hendrix was born and grew up in Seattle and is celebrated on the sidewalk close to Broadway Crossing with a sculpture of him playing his guitar. Cha-cha-cha dance steps embedded on the sidewalk at Broadway Crossing reinforce social cohesion with other areas in the Capitol Hill neighbourhood, whose dance steps are for the rhumba, foxtrot and tango. As is the case in LGBT areas of many other US cities, the Capitol Hill neighbourhood asserts its liberal ethos with rainbow-coloured crossings at principal street intersections. These examples typify the meaning that can be invested when a community has built up its own strong identity that can be passed on to future generations.

# CASE STUDY 3.6.2
# 'INCREDIBLE EDIBLE', TODMORDEN, CALDERDALE, UK

## INSPIRATIONAL LEADERSHIP

'If you eat, you're in'.[10] This is one of the many catchphrases dreamed up by Mary Clear and Pam Warhurst, founders of 'Incredible Edible' in 2008. Its heart is in Todmorden in the Upper Calder Valley, Yorkshire, also known as Calderdale, but the chords it has struck have resonated in hundreds of places around the world where communities have been inspired to create their own versions of the concept.

Calderdale is very beautiful, and Todmorden is one of line of well-established settlements nestling along the River Calder and the Rochdale Canal, hemmed in by steep-sided, wooded hills. Its heritage dates from the Industrial Revolution in the 19th century, with the establishment of mills to serve the textile industry that was developing around the Manchester conurbation to the west and Halifax, Bradford and Leeds to the east.

When overseas competition during the second half of the 20th century caused Calderdale's textile industry to dwindle, the community was determined to find a way to make a new start, and was supported by the government-funded 'Yorkshire Renaissance', part of 'Yorkshire Forward'. Their 'no holds barred' approach speaks for itself, with its captivating, warm-hearted and inclusive message that opened-up possibilities surpassing any expectations their audiences may have had.

## ADDRESSING THE CHALLENGE

Clear explained: 'Things weren't going so well in the world, but we didn't want to feel like victims, so Pam and I got talking and she said she likes cooking and I said I like eating.'[11] One of their strategies was the bold, direct action of not asking for permission to do something they believed to be harmless and important, which they rationalised on the basis that they knew they could always apologise. They used this as justification to go ahead with 'guerrilla gardening', growing food on neglected patches of green space, and this generated a group of enthusiastic volunteers. Encouraged by such support they asked permission from the local authority to dig up ornamental flower beds in the town's public spaces and replace them with vegetables. When objections were raised that food in such locations would be too contaminated to eat, they engaged in research whose conclusion was that humans are hard-wired not to destroy food: 'no one pees on a parsnip'!

A planting schedule of ornamental trees for a health centre under construction led them to approach the doctors who agreed they could plant fruit trees instead, meaning that waiting patients could pick and eat healthy fruit. Concerns about people stealing food grown in public areas were answered with 'you can't steal something that's free' and 'sharing sets a good precedent'. The word 'KINDNESS' writ large in public places, including on a planter next to the railway station, prompted commuters to bring scissors and bags into which they could put fresh herbs to take home.

**FIGURE 3.6.12** The Incredible Todmorden Way! A statement of intent

**FIGURE 3.6.13** Growing food on streets – using urban space productively

## HELPING ONE ANOTHER

These are just the tip of the iceberg of initiatives that have taken place over the last decade, and the way the community has been re-inventing itself was demonstrated by the high turn-out at the 'Incredible Festival of Ideas' in June 2018. Shared between Todmorden and Hebden Bridge, 5 miles to the east, well-attended events included the 'Handmade Parade', for which the police blocked the valley's only through-road several times in the course of 45 minutes to give priority to the huge procession of enormous puppets and gaily-outfitted groups of local people.

In terms of what empowers communities, it is interesting to see how, managed the right way, unity can grow out of adversity, perhaps akin to 'war-spirit'.

As well as the loss of its employment base, in recent years Calderdale has been suffering from extreme flooding due to the combination of its steep-sided topography and periods of increasingly intense rainfall. Despite the massive disruption this causes, residents and businesses are willing to put up with it because of their attachment to the combination of the location and the people who live there, that together make it such a special place. A 'Resilience Workshop' was part of the 'Incredible Festival of Ideas' in which participants presented a wide range of creative ideas on ways to overcome the many problems. It included poignant testimonies to the distress local people had experienced and examples of the customised therapies being provided to help

**FIGURE 3.6.14** Handmade Parade – the community enjoying serious play

**FIGURE 3.6.15** Handmade Parade stops traffic – having the right priorities

them cope with the psychological challenges of rebuilding their lives. The communication processes through which participants learned about the difficulties of other attendees was itself therapeutic.

## COMMUNITY IDENTITY

Calderdale's somewhat isolated setting in such a dramatic valley gives it an identity one might assume would in itself generate a sense of community. Whilst this is to some extent the case, it nonetheless turns out that each of the separate settlements tends to adhere to its own identity, as opposed to basking in a collective harmony. This may be the sense in which difference and diversity can be an essential ingredient in keeping communities healthy, allowing them to innovate and evolve over time.

Clear and Warhurst are exceptional, inspirational individuals with the talents and skills to create and communicate this form of community empowerment, gently conscripting a willing army of local people who will support the cause because of the way it increases their sense of collaboration and purpose. It raises the question as to whether people with the same potential to address important issues and inspire others to join them are to be found in every neighbourhood. Examples such as Incredible Edible at least show what can be done.

## CHAPTER 4

# WHERE NEXT?

*'Nothing dates so quickly as predictions of the future.'*[1]

**ROBERT HUGHES**

# INTRODUCTION

Our future and that of the planet is uncertain and unpredictable. Technology does not alter people's basic needs and 21st-century progress combines major advances with unexpected consequences. City centre space continues to be at a premium and too much emphasis is placed on shopping as opposed to the overall experience of spending time in the public realm.

This chapter suggests some possible factors to consider that relate to our collective awareness regarding the predicament in which we find ourselves: Generational change, new types of settlement and where to build.

## GENERATIONAL CHANGE

Millennials in cities seem to be less interested in car ownership than baby boomers and have more flexible attitudes to mobility options. As they tend to see cars as expensive, they show less urgency to learn to drive and are comfortable using the growing number of alternative forms of mobility: taking the bus, tram or tube, walking, cycling, using scooters, car-sharing, Zip-cars, Uber, taxis, minicabs and car rental for longer journeys, all assisted by their fluency in using the internet and navigation apps.

Many city dwellers see a car as a responsibility and a burden rather than an asset, and new residential developments in cities are increasingly required not to provide residents' parking, which often reduces the amount of objection locally. In lower density environments, where cars are the norm, traffic congestion is typically the major cause of local opposition to proposals.

The possibility of significant reductions in private car ownership has been considered in the future-orientated design of a car park in Cincinnati, USA, Cincinnati 84.51 by KLH Engineers. The innovative project has been built as a multi-storey car park but with its floor to floor heights and other technical specifications allowing space for the future requirements of commercial office structures. Although the construction costs will have been far higher than those of a standard multi-storey, payback on the investment is planned for a future in which there is a groundswell amongst enlightened citizens recognising the benefits of reductions in private car use. The logic is for the parking space to be converted into offices, starting from the top storey and working its way down, retaining whatever parking or other service spaces are needed on lower floors. The building itself is consequently more attractive than traditional multi-storey car parks.

## NEW TYPES OF SETTLEMENT AND WHERE TO BUILD

The initiative for garden towns and villages represents a reawakening of Ebenezer Howard's Garden City concept. Typically located in rural areas, opposition from local people may be substantial – above all due to their expectation of traffic congestion on top of what they already experience (and contribute to). The more open-minded recognise that a significant increase in local population can make public transport more viable and run regularly enough to ease the current situation.

The deficits, over several decades, in UK housing supply have led to often polarised debates over the advantages of incursions into areas of green belt as opposed to first making use of all available urban brownfield sites. Considered through the lens of healthy placemaking, the following points come to the fore:

- There is unlikely to be enough urban brownfield land in the right places to satisfy overall housing demand.
- The more density that is packed into the urban environment, the more need there is for accessible urban green space, of all kinds.
- There are many other concerns about the quality of life in what some critics see as over-dense environments, at present being pushed to one side by the extreme level of demand to live, and invest, in urban centres.
- Environmentalists have recognised that urban brownfield sites left untouched for many years generate high levels of biodiversity – far more than in many areas of agricultural land in the green belt where the production of food takes place. In other words, not all green belt is green. Industrial-scale farming is often detrimental to the environment, for instance due to the spraying of harmful pesticides and the leaching of fertilisers into ecosystems.

- Honeybees are known to thrive in many urban locations, visiting the flowers people plant in their gardens and window boxes, whereas modern farming practices have slashed the populations of these free pollinators by decimating the wild-flower meadows in the countryside on which the bees depend.
- Greenery inside the city contributes to urban cooling whereas more buildings add to the urban heat island effect.

The healthy placemaking response to this scenario would be a rational strategy, perhaps at odds with short-term economic gain but fully aligned with long-term sustainability and environmental governance:

- To retain strategically-located brownfield sites that are green, and enhance them to serve as public amenity spaces in existing high-density residential neighbourhoods.
- To permit green belt development in the form of sustainable settlements, perhaps Garden Towns and Villages, where greenfield land has little prospect of contributing to environmental quality.
- The location of green belt settlements in terms of transport connections would have to be considered with great care. The short-term demand for ever more people to commute into urban centres would exacerbate the problems of our already overstretched transport networks. But a longer-term strategy could overcome this, whereby the mixed uses make these settlements more self-sufficient and independent, not least because they would be close to centres of sustainably farmed food production.
- It would also be essential to ensure that the presence of these new settlements in the former green belt would not damage the high quality green space nearby.
- The design of such settlements would be required to adhere to all the principles of healthy placemaking, and at all costs avoid becoming low-density, car-dependent, commuter enclaves.

## PUSHING ON AN OPEN DOOR?

There are encouraging signs that the importance of healthy placemaking is gaining recognition at many levels, in particular amongst the younger generations, and being implemented in settlements of all sizes and in many countries.

New factors emerge and are overtaken by others at an ever-increasing rate and so it is important to allow enough flexibility for developments to adapt for a future that we cannot predict. Planning for them has its risks, but history has shown that, in spite of societal and technological change, people seem to be content with traditional urban structures that enable them to have a good experience when going about their daily lives.

The explosion of technological advances in the first half of the 20th century inspired the Modernist movement with its 'Brave New World' ambition to re-think people's lives and make cities as rational as machines. The legacy of these ideas continued during the second half of the 20th century. The outcomes have been mixed and many have not lived up to what the visionaries had intended, perhaps because the polemics were so persuasive and exciting for them to have been insufficiently questioned.

People have become intoxicated by the lifestyle now on offer, despite the fact that we now live in the 'Anthropocene Epoch' where *Homo sapiens* is the strongest force changing the geology of our planet. Whilst technology is scientific and has progressed in ways that have transformed our lives, this has obscured the fact that humans are still human. Societal development has not, and cannot, keep pace with the rate of innovation and the power of multinational organisations wielding untold wealth.

Progressive city planners around the world are narrowing roads and dismantling one-way systems and gyratories. They are restoring urban structures to their former logic as spaces to be shared by all users, and not just mechanisms to speed motor vehicles on their way. In London, the Congestion Charge and expensive parking fees are helping to rebalance the way urban space is used, and the gains in quality, vibrancy and economic energy are enough for people to forego the 'luxury' of driving into the city centre.

People continue to be comfortable at a human scale and are happy to mingle in stimulating, mixed-use public spaces, as the Modernist ethos of zoned uses is being superseded by a return to the more interesting and stimulating 'muddled use of land'.

If all aspects of people's lives and their health were in good order there would have been no need to write this book, and if the message was not somewhat controversial there would be no point in having written it. The number of stones as yet unturned is immense so it is reassuring to realise how much all of us can do, as individuals and collectively, to improve people's health and quality of life.

Modern life is complicated and the structure of urban environments can make it harder to keep all the plates spinning. Circumstances can make some challenges unavoidable but others can be choices that depend on how we prioritise different aspects of our lives. In setting out the key issues, this book has tried to explain some of the reasoning behind them and the connections between them. Individually, the issues may be self-evident but the business of balancing their complexities is an ongoing process.

Healthy placemaking is an elusive topic because it touches almost every aspect of our lives and every decision we make. None of the adjustments recommended can deliver quick or dramatic transformations but, harnessed together, their combined effects can lead to substantial improvements to our quality of life. Making the right decisions is difficult, not only for individuals but also for urban planners working with health professionals on strategies to produce the best outcomes for the wider public.

Overcoming challenges to help us feel in control of our environment is life-enhancing. The evidence regarding the urban planning challenges we face speaks for itself and points to realistic remedies within our grasp. This puts us in a position to make step by step progress towards the improvement of health and wellbeing using as a basis the framework set out by the principles of healthy placemaking.

# REFERENCES

## INTRODUCTION

1   https://www.who.int/about/who-we-are/constitution
2   'Life expectancy', Global Health Observatory data, https://www.who.int/gho/mortality_burden_disease/life_tables/situation_trends_text/en/ (accessed May 2019)
3   Kira M. Newman, 'Six Ways Happiness Is Good for Your Health', *Greater Good Magazine*, 2015
4   'Every breath we take: the lifelong impact of air pollution', Royal College of Physicians, 2016, p. 2
5   Ibid

## CHAPTER 1

1   L. Carmichael, 'Healthy cities: the evidence and what to do with it', *Urban Design Group Journal Spring* 2017, issue 142, pp. 20-22
2   Alan A. Jackson, *Semi-Detached London: Suburban Development, Life and Transport*, 1900-39, London, Allen & Unwin, 1973
3   E.J Carter and Ernö Goldfinger, *The County of London Plan*, London, Penguin Books, 1945
4   Ibid, p. 51
5   Ibid, p. 48
6   'City Planning and population health: a global challenge', *The Lancet*, 2016, volume 388, issue 10062, p. 2917
7   World Health Organization, 'Global action plan on physical activity 2018-2030', 2018, p. 67
8   'Food system challenges', *Food Foundation*, https://foodfoundation.org.uk/food-system-challenges/ (accessed May 2019)
9   *Sustainable Development Goals in the UK follow up: Hunger, malnutrition and food insecurity in the UK,* House of Commons Environmental Audit Committee, 2019, https://publications.parliament.uk/pa/cm201719/cmselect/cmenvaud/1491/1491.pdf (accessed May 2019)
10  'Every breath we take: the lifelong impact of air pollution', Royal College of Physicians, 2016, p. xii
11  'In-car air pollution', *IQ Air*, https://www.iqair.com/international/blog/air-quality/in-car-pollution (accessed May 2019)
12  Sandra Laville, 'Ella Kissi-Debrah: a new inquest granted into "air pollution" death', *The Guardian*, 2019, https://www.theguardian.com/uk-news/2019/may/02/ella-kissi-debrah-new-inquest-granted-into-air-pollution-death (accessed May 2019)
13  Helen Kingston, 'Frome – an experience of building a more compassionate community', *South West Clinical Network*, 2016, http://www.swscn.org.uk/wp/wp-content/uploads/2015/07/Community-development-in-Frome-the-GP-perspective-Dr-Helen-Kingston.pdf (accessed May 2019)
14  George Monbiot, 'The town that's found a potent cure for illness – community', *The Guardian*, 2018, https://www.theguardian.com/commentisfree/2018/feb/21/town-cure-illness-community-frome-somerset-isolation (accessed May 2019)
15  'Analysis of walking potential 2016', *Transport for London*, 2017, http://content.tfl.gov.uk/analysis-of-walking-potential-2016.pdf (accessed May 2019)
16  'Physical activity guidelines for adults', NHS, https://www.nhs.uk/live-well/exercise/ (accessed May 2019)
17  Alvin Powell, 'Humans hot, sweaty, natural-born runners', https://news.harvard.edu/gazette/story/2007/04/humans-hot-sweaty-natural-born-runners/ (accessed August 2019)
18  'Benefits of exercise', NHS, https://www.nhs.uk/live-well/exercise/exercise-health-benefits/ (accessed May 2019)
19  David Roberts, 'Lessons on urbanism from a Vancouver veteran', *Vox*, 2018, https://www.vox.com/2017/6/20/15828464/urbanism-brent-toderian (accessed May 2019)
20  'Every breath we take: the lifelong impact of air pollution', Royal College of Physicians, 2016, p. 39
21  'A guide to setting up a park and stride scheme', Living Streets, https://www.livingstreets.org.uk/media/2035/park-and-stride-print.pdf (accessed May 2019)
22  Howard Frumkin, 'Our Planet, our Health', SALUS Health City Design conference, 2018
23  'Every breath we take: the lifelong impact of air pollution', Royal College of Physicians, 2016, p. 92
24  'City Planning and population health: a global challenge', *The Lancet*, 2016, volume 388, issue 10062, pp. 2912-2924
25  Nicholas Stern, *The Economics of Climate Change*, Cambridge University Press, 2006, p. vii
26  'Every breath we take: the lifelong impact of air pollution', Royal College of Physicians, 2016, p. 92

## CHAPTER 2

1   David Roberts, 'Lessons on urbanism from a Vancouver veteran', *Vox*, 2018, https://www.vox.com/2017/6/20/15828464/urbanism-brent-toderian (accessed May 2019)
2   Harry Quilter-Pinner and Laurie Laybourn-Langton, 'Lethal and illegal: London's air pollution crisis', *IPPR*, 2016 http://www.ippr.org/publications/lethal-and-illegal-londons-air-pollution-crisis (accessed May 2019)
3   'Analysing air pollution exposure in London', Greater London Authority, 2017, https://data.london.gov.uk/dataset/analysing-air-pollution-exposure-in-london (accessed May 2019)

4   Dr Rachel Bragg, Dr Carly Wood, Dr Jo Barton and Professor Jules Pretty, 'Health and wellbeing benefits of contact with nature', *Wellbeing benefits from natural environments rich in wildlife*, University of Essex for The Wildlife Trusts, 2015, pp. 13-17

5   Center for Active Design, *Assembly: Civic Design Guidelines*, New York, 2018, p. 92

6   Ibid

7   https://www.securedbydesign.com

8   'Ghent: a child and youth-friendly city', *Ghent International*, 2015, https://stad.gent/ghent-international/city-policy/ghent-child-and-youth-friendly-city (accessed May 2019)

9   Fabijana Popovic, 'Healthy Cities are built on purpose', Gehl Blog, 2014

10  European Environment Agency, 'Managing Exposure to Noise in Europe', 2017, p. 1

11  Stephen A. Stanfield and Mark P. Matheson, 'Noise pollution; non-auditory effects on health', *British Medical Bulletin*, 68 (1), 2003, pp. 243-257

12  C.A. Wyse et al, 'Circadian desynchrony and metabolic disfunction: Did light pollution make us fat?', *Medical Hypotheses*, 77 (6), 2011, pp. 1139-1144

13  Christine Ro, 'How to cure the eco-anxious', *Wellcome Trust*, 2018, https://wellcomecollection.org/articles/Ww2BOCEAAMsAioTE (accessed May 2019)

14  Neville Owen, 'Sedentary behavior: understanding and influencing adults' prolonged sitting time', *Preventive Medicine*, 55 (6), 2012, pp. 535-39

15  David Israelson, 'Why walkable cities are a step ahead', *Globe Investor*, 2012

16  Howard Frumkin, 'Our Planet, our Health', SALUS Health City Design conference, 2018

# CHAPTER 3

1   Transport for London, 'Getting more people walking and cycling could help save our high streets', 2018

2   Bettina Thoma-Schade, 'Visiting Kenya a year into its plastic bag ban', *DW*, 2018, https://www.dw.com/en/visiting-kenya-a-year-into-its-plastic-bag-ban/a-45254144 (accessed May 2019)

## CHAPTER 3.1

1   Jane Jacobs, *The Death and Life of Great American Cities*, Modern Library Edition, 1993, p. 5

2   UN Habitat, 'Planning and design for sustainable urban mobility', 2013

3   Jeff Tumlin, *Sustainable Transportation Planning*, San Francisco, Wiley & Sons Inc, 2012, p. 46

4   Ibid.

5   David Roberts, 'Lessons on urbanism from a Vancouver veteran', *Vox*, 2018, https://www.vox.com/2017/6/20/15828464/urbanism-brent-toderian (accessed May 2019)

6   UN Habitat, 'Planning and design for sustainable urban mobility', 2013

7   'Traffic congestion cost UK motorists over £37.7 billion in 2016', *INRIX*, http://inrix.com/press-releases/scorecard-2017-uk/ (accessed May 2019)

## CHAPTER 3.2

1   David Israelson, 'Why walkable cities are a step ahead', *Globe Investor*, 2012

2   Living Streets, 'The Pedestrian Pound', 2014, p. 10

3   Sophie Tyler, Giles Semper, Peter Guest and Ben Fieldhouse, 'The relevance of parking in the success of urban centres', 2012, p. 5

4   Living Streets, 'The Pedestrian Pound', 2014, p. 10

## CHAPTER 3.3

1   Saffron Woodcraft, 'City Streets: Urban Innovation on a Human Scale Social Life', *Social Life*

2   'City Planning and population health: a global challenge', *The Lancet*, 2016, volume 388, issue 10062

3   William H. Whyte, *The social life of small urban spaces*, Washington DC, Conservation Foundation, 1980, p. 1

4   Jennifer Kent and Susan Thompson, 'Connecting and strengthening communities', *Australian Planner*, 51 (3), 2013, p. 58

## CHAPTER 3.4

1   David Pencheon, SALUS Healthy City Design Conference, 2017

2   World Health Organization, 'Global action plan on physical activity 2018-2030', 2018, p. 6

3   Fabijana Popovic, 'Healthy Cities are built on purpose', Gehl Blog, 2014

4   Nicole Badstruber, 'London congestion charge: what worked, what didn't, what next', *The Conversation*, 2018, https://theconversation.com/london-congestion-charge-why-its-time-to-reconsider-one-of-the-citys-great-successes-92478 (accessed May 2019)

5   Living Streets, 'The Pedestrian Pound', 2014, pp. 28-32

6   Shane Turner, R. Singh, P. Quinn and T. Allatt, 'Benefits of new and improved pedestrian facilities – before and after studies', New Zealand Transport Agency, 2011, p. 436

7   Jeff Tumlin, Sustainable Transportation Planning, San Francisco, Wiley & Sons Inc, 2012, p. 49

8   Joseph Goodman, Melissa Laube and Judith Schwenk, 'Issues in bus rapid transit', *Federal Transit Administration*, 2005-6, https://www.transit.dot.gov/sites/fta.dot.gov/files/issues.pdf (accessed May 2019)

9   Richard Mazuch and David McKenna, 'Anatomy of Healthy Spaces: Insights and Solutions', Healthy City Design, 2018

10  'Pedestrian barriers – safety's friend or community's foe?', Free Wheel North, 2016, https://www.freewheelnorth.org.uk/single-post/2016/08/05/Pedestrian-Barriers-Safety%E2%80%99s-Friend-or-Community%E2%80%99s-Foe (accessed May 2019)

11  http://www.20splenty.org/

12  Hans-Jürgen Best, Stadtdirektor (Chief Planner) of Essen, quoted on Von Zadow's website

13  Ian Birrell, 'America's most overweight cities: how Oklahoma is battling obesity', Independent, 2015, https://www.independent.co.uk/life-style/health-and-families/features/americas-most-overweight-cities-how-oklahoma-is-battling-obesity-a6721901.html (accessed May 2019)

## CHAPTER 3.5

1   Herbert Dreiseitl, 'Blue-green social placemaking', Journal of Urban Regeneration and Renewal, Volume 8 Number 2: Winter 2014-15, pp. 161-170

2   Kelsey Campbell-Dollaghan, 'The case for building $1,500 parks', Fast Company, 2018, https://www.fastcompany.com/90206556/the-case-for-building-1500-parks (accessed May 2019)

3   Ibid.

4   Richard Kenny, 'Paris: a city that is turning streets into gardens', BBC World Hacks, 2018, https://www.bbc.co.uk/news/av/stories-46275458/paris-a-city-that-is-turning-streets-into-gardens (accessed May 2019)

5   Harry Burns, 'Wellness not illness: why place matters for health', in Growing Awareness: how green consciousness can change perceptions and places, ed. Brian and Sue Evans, RIAS Publications, Edinburgh, 2016

6   Amy Kolczack, 'This city aims to be the world's greenest', National Geographic, 2017, https://www.nationalgeographic.com/environment/urban-expeditions/green-buildings/green-urban-landscape-cities-Singapore/ (accessed May 2019)

7   Margaret Poet, 'Biophillic design is king at this Singapore hospital', gb&d magazine, 2018, https://gbdmagazine.com/2018/singapore-hospital/ (accessed May 2019)

8   Amy Frearson, 'PARKROYAL on pickering by WOHA', Dezeen, 2013, https://www.dezeen.com/2013/10/10/parkroyal-on-pickering-by-woha/ (accessed May 2019)

9   Natasha Kwok, 'WOHA's Oasia hotel conceived as a living green tower in downtown Singapore, designboom, 2016, https://www.designboom.com/architecture/woha-oasia-hotel-downtown-singapore-living-tower-12-07-2016/ (accessed May 2019)

10  'Parks and green spaces', Transport for London, https://www.london.gov.uk//what-we-do/environment/parks-green-spaces-and-biodiversity/parks-and-green-spaces (accessed May 2019)

## CHAPTER 3.6

1   Jim Diers, 'Neighborhoods mini-summit', Seattle Neighborhood Coalition, 2016

2   Definition of community, Merriam Webster, https://www.merriam-webster.com/dictionary/community (accessed May 2019)

3   'What is asset based community development?', DePaul University, https://resources.depaul.edu/abcd-institute/resources/Documents/WhatisAssetBasedCommunityDevelopment.pdf (accessed May 2019)

4   https://www.timebanking.org/

5   Charles Campion, 20/20 Visions – Collaborative Planning and Placemaking, London, RIBA Publishing, 2018

6   'Collaborative Planning For All', Civic Voice, 2015

7   Joel Mills, Director of 'Communities by Design' American Institute of Architects

8   Kay Rood, 'Creating Cal Anderson Park', History Link, 2006, http://www.historylink.org/File/7603 (accessed May 2019)

9   Ibid.

10  Mary Clear and Pam Warhurst https://www.incredibleedible.org.uk/

11  Mary Clear, personal correspondence, 2019

## CHAPTER 4

1   Robert Hughes, The Shock of the New, London, Thames & Hudson, 1991

# IMAGE CREDITS

Figures 1.1–2 – Fred London; Figure 2.1 – Rolf Messerschmidt; Figures 3.0.1–5 – Fred London; Figures 3.1.1–16 – Fred London; Figure 3.2.1a – JTP; Figure 3.2.1b – Gillespies and JTP; Figure 3.2.2 – Fred London; Figure 3.2.3a – JTP; Figure 3.2.3b – Gillespies and JTP; Figures 3.2.4–12 – Fred London; Figure 3.2.13 – Herbert Dreiseitl; Figures 3.2.14–15 – Fred London; Figure 3.2.16 – Google Earth; Figures 3.2.17–21 – Fred London; Figures 3.3.1–2 – Fred London; Figure 3.3.3 – Wikimedia commons; Figures 3.3.4–6 – Fred London; Figure 3.3.7 – Alkis Tzavaras, JTP; Figures 3.3.8–15 – Fred London; Figures 3.4.1–5 – Fred London; Figures 3.4.6a and b – Euroluftbild and JTP; Figures 3.4.7–10 – OJB Landscape architecture; Figures 3.5.1–5 – Fred London; Figure 3.5.6 – Herbert Dreiseitl; Figures 3.5.7–8 Ramboll Images Singapore; Figure 3.5.9 – Herbert Dreiseitl; Figure 3.5.10 – Carl Patten; Figures 3.5.11–13 – Herbert Dreiseitl; Figures 3.5.14–18 – Fred London; Figures 3.6.1–5 – JTP; Figure 3.6.6 – Kay Rood; Figure 3.6.7 – Jim Diers; Figures 3.6.8–15 – Fred London.

# INDEX

Page numbers in **bold** indicate tables and in *italic* indicate figures.